One with God

What it is like to be with God, a chronicle of spiritual growth after my near-death experiences.

Darrin Pelley

One With God
Copyright © 2022 by Darrin Pelley

All rights reserved. No part of this book may be reproduced or used in any manner without written permission of the copyright owner except for the use of quotations in a book review. For more information, address: dwpelley@msn.com

Darrin Pelley, 1970-
One with God: What it is like to be with God, a chronicle of spiritual growth after my near-death experiences

ISBN 979-8-9876455-0-5 Paperback
ISBN 979-8-9876455-1-2 Hardback
ISBN 979-8-9876455-2-9 eBook

Unless otherwise marked, Scripture quotations are taken from the *The Holy Bible, English Standard Version*® (ESV®).
Copyright © 2001 by Crossway, a publishing ministry of Good News Publishers. All rights reserved.

Edited by Tiffany Shand
Cover Design by Germancreative
Interior Design and typeset by Aslishaa

Contents

Part 1: What I Know and How I Know It 1

    Chapter 1: God Loves You Very Much 3

    Chapter 2: My Life Before Christ 16

    Chapter 3: From Six to Thirty and Encountering God 28

Part 2: Elements of Faith 43

    Chapter 4: Receiving Salvation and Forgiveness 45

    Chapter 5: Forgiving and Loving Others 53

    Chapter 6: Prayer 78

    Conclusion: Love is Everything 127

    Bibliography 129

Part 1

What I Know and How I Know It

Chapter 1
God Loves You Very Much

All your problems in life come from one simple source.

You do not know how much God loves you.

No, you don't.

I can hear you arguing with me, but I've met thousands of Christians and non Christians alike. Hardly any of them know this fundamental fact of reality. **God loves you very much.** That is an understatement.

God. Loves. You. Very. Much. Even punctuated this way, it is an understatement. Let me try some other ways: God is crazy about you. God is wild for you. God is in love with you. The Song of Songs in the Bible is a racy book (as far as books of the Bible go). It's a love story that seems to be about Solomon and his love affair with a princess whom he married. We could all learn a thing or two about romance from this mysterious Bible text. But the ancient Church Fathers always saw the romantic love of the Song of Songs as a metaphor for God's love for his people. Within the first few verses of the opening stanza, it says,

> 2 Let him kiss me with the kisses of his mouth—
> For your love is better than wine.
> 3 Because of the fragrance of your good ointments,

> Your name is ointment poured forth;
> Therefore the virgins love you.
> 4 Draw me away! (SS 1:2-4 NKJV).

It makes most people uncomfortable to think about this. I think that is probably what it is supposed to do.

The emotional power of romantic love does help us understand the love of God. But we must also understand the parental love of God for us. I saw a quote in a book called *Horns* by an author named Joe Hill: "I mean, when the world comes for your children, with the knives out, it's your job to stand in the way." That's a powerful image. Thinking of God as a protective and loving Father helps us to understand this dimension of his love, especially if you had such a father, or you are one.

But eventually, you are going to see that the only way to comprehend the love God has for you is to consider the cross.

For now, though, I will simply and blithely say, *God loves you very much.*

I know you don't understand this, because you aren't overwhelmed by the fact. You aren't dancing for joy with your arms up in a victory pose, praising him and filling up on the great truth of his love! You don't get it, and that's ok. After reading this book, I am hoping you totally understand it, 100%, in every fiber of your being.

Love for Everyone

I know you don't get it, because if you did, you would love everyone, no matter who, no matter what they've done to you. You would love everyone with the love of God. You wouldn't' have to try. You couldn't help it. If I'm wrong about you, and you understand this already, forgive me. But please keep reading. We can all love God *even more* deeply by knowing the truth of his love for us. That is my goal in this book. I want you to know what I have been blessed to know.

If you are like many people, you had a grandmother who loved you unconditionally. This is why kids love their nanas, mimis, grandmas, or whatever they called her. Grandmas are pure joy, acceptance, and generosity, in most peoples' experience. If at least one of your grandmothers wasn't like that, I'm truly sorry. Imagine that is how you felt about your grandmother. Now, imagine that someone told you she had died. You are distraught. You realize you didn't go and see her last summer when you had planned to, because you got busy. You realize that there are a million things you wish you would have asked her. You are sitting there crying in sorrow, because you already miss her so much. Imagine it until you feel what that would be like. Even imagine that you had heard she had suffered, asking for you, and you had not known, or you would have gone.

Terrible, isn't it?

Now imagine you are packing your bags, getting ready to get on a plane to go to your grandmother's funeral. You are still very sad. You go to the airport, check in, settle in on a flight, still thinking about what you would miss about your grandmother. You just realized this will be the first Christmas without her. Where is everyone going to gather this year? Next month will be your birthday, but you won't get a card from her. As you sit on the plane, you are just plain sad.

You finally land and rent your car, where you must drive two hours in utter heartache, wondering how you are going to get through the next two days with your family, who will all be having one of the worst moments of their lives. You're usually the strong one, but you don't feel strong as you drive, remembering every hug, every kindness, just that warm smile of love and acceptance that you won't see again. As you drive, you see all the familiar landmarks that used to thrill you as a child, because it meant you were getting close to Grandma's house. Now you know this might be the very last time you make this drive. You are sobbing.

Imagine that you get to her house, and the door opens.

And it's her.

It's her, alive and well. You don't know why someone said she had died, but here she is, just fine.

When she warmly embraces you, you can feel how strong she still is, and you know that she has a lot of years left in her…a lot of Christmases, birthdays, hugs, unconditional acceptance, and everything else that comes with a wonderful grandma. Think of how relieved you are. Think of the love that fills your heart. Imagine that love permeating every cell of your body. Imagine that it is like light bursting forth from you, so that you are lit up like an angel. It is pure rapture and delight beyond comprehension. It is a feeling of acceptance and pleasure that is unparalleled right when you need it most.

That is something like a minuscule fraction of what it feels like in God's love, but honestly, it doesn't even compare.

God is pure love.

In the Bible, St. John, who Scripture calls "the disciple that Jesus loved," tells us that "God is love." Think about that. What is more wonderful than love when it is returned? I know that the unrequited love of the poets and songwriters is a powerful feeling, but I'm talking about love that is returned.

God is love, pure love. The only thing that comes close to helping us understand this love is what John says about it in his first letter. You know about John 3:16, "For God so loved the world that he gave his one and only Son, that whoever believes in him shall not perish but have eternal life."

But do you know about 1 John 3:16? "This is how we know what love is: Jesus Christ laid down his life for us. And we ought to lay down our lives for our brothers and sisters" (NIV).

Jesus Christ "laid down his life for us." That is such an understatement! I guess we could try to illustrate it by going back to our grandmother situation. Our dear, loving grandma is still alive. Why? What if it turned out that someone loved her so much that when they heard about a way to take her place in death, they volunteered against her will? They loved her so much that they offered themselves as a substitute. That's love!

But Jesus did more than that. He gave his life for people, not because they were so good, but because in terms of sin, they were actually bad. I'll write more about this later, but Jesus gave his life for us when we did not deserve it, when we hated him. That is pure unconditional love!

How I Know

I know that God is real, that Jesus is God the Son sent to die on the cross for you and me. I know his love because of this. But I also know his love because I have been given an amazing blessing. I have a condition, an actual, life-long illness. It is not a major diagnosis or an extremely intolerable disease but a platform through which I know things most people do not, and for that I am truly grateful and blessed. What's the condition? *I am a type one diabetic.*

You may not think such a thing is a blessing, and neither did I for a long time. In fact, I could only see it as a curse. Why, at nine years old did I have to find out I was a diabetic? Why did I have to grow up so fast, knowing that if I didn't take on the enormous responsibility of taking care of myself—administering blood tests and insulin injections, and monitoring my diet, stress and exercise every single day—I might die? Why did I have to give up the carefree childhood that my friends had?

I did not know the answer then, but I do now.

Something happened. It didn't just happen once, but again and again! Simply put, during different diabetic episodes where my blood sugar had gone way too low, I experienced the presence of God. If you will keep reading, I'll explain this in a later chapter. For now, just know that I have been somewhere that most people don't go until they die. Since this happened, I can only see my disease as a gift that I wouldn't trade for all the world. Trust me!

Maximillion Kolbe

Perhaps you know the facts about Jesus' death on the cross for you. Maybe you grew up hearing about the gospel, so it doesn't have quite the impact that it should. Or maybe it once blew you away, but now you're so used to the idea that it fails to move you anymore. I want to illustrate it for you by telling you a story of something that happened during WWII in a Nazi death camp.

Maximillion Kolbe (1894-1941) was a Polish Catholic Priest and a Franciscan Friar. He was converted to Christ at the age of twelve when he was given a vision of the Virgin Mary. In his words:

> That night I asked the Mother of God what was to become of me. Then she came to me holding two crowns, one white, the other red. She asked me if I was willing to accept either of these crowns. The white one meant that I should persevere in purity and the red that I should become a martyr. I said that I would accept them both. (Armstrong, Regis J.; Peterson, Ingrid J. (2010). The Franciscan Tradition. Liturgical Press. p. 50. ISBN 978-0-8146-3922-1.)

A few years later, he took orders and was ordained a priest and monk. He served the Church in various ways, starting monasteries in Poland and Japan, a publishing operation, and a radio station. By the time of WWII, he was sheltering refugees from Poland in the monastery, 2000 of whom were Jews. He was one of the few friars to remain after the Nazi occupation, and he spent his hours publishing anti-Nazi literature and hiding Jews from capture. He was arrested again, and on May 28th, he was sent to Auschwitz.

While he was imprisoned there, he went about his priestly duties, preaching, hearing confessions, and administering whatever they could use for sacraments. Kolbe was harassed violently by the guards and beaten regularly. Then one day, a man attempted to escape the prison and was caught. In response, the deputy commander elected to put ten men in an underground bunker to starve to death as a way to discourage anyone else from attempting escape. They chose ten, and when one of them cried, "My wife! My children!" Kolbe intervened and volunteered for the man's position.

Can you imagine this? Would you have done that? He said, "I don't have a wife and kids. I'll take his place." I don't know if he even knew the man, but the fact that the story happened so recently in history and in a place that we've learned so much about, Auschwitz, helps me to *feel* something about the sacrifice of one for the life of another. "By this we know love…" If unconditional love can be measured, this is the place to start, the cross. Jesus Christ died for all.

While inside the bunker, Kolbe continued to minister to the others. Whenever the guards looked in, they found him kneeling in prayer or sitting before the other men, calmly looking at the guard who entered. After two weeks of no food or water, Kolbe was the only man left alive, the other nine having died. The guards decided to give him a lethal injection in one arm. He raised his other arm to God as he perished. Maximillion Kolbe was canonized in 1982.

The night that Christ was betrayed, he prayed because he was afraid. Jesus was fully human, and he felt as deeply as anyone. In Luke 22:41-44, it says,

> 41 And he withdrew from them about a stone's throw, and knelt down and prayed, 42 saying, "Father, if you are willing, remove this cup from me. Nevertheless, not my will, but yours, be done." 43 And there appeared to him an angel from heaven, strengthening him. 44 And being in agony he prayed more earnestly; and his sweat became like great drops of blood falling down to the ground. (ESV)

He was not excited about the suffering that awaited him. He was to be betrayed by his friend, abandoned by everyone, disowned by Peter. He was going to be mocked, beaten, spit on, tortured mercilessly, and finally, crucified, which led to a painful death by asphyxiation when one could no longer hold up his weight on the nails in his feet and hands. It was horrific, and Jesus was in no doubt about what it would be like for him. But as theologian John Stott pointed out, that wasn't what Jesus was most concerned about. What caused him to sweat blood was the certainty that he would bear the sin of the world, and that his Father would be forced to abandon him at that hour. Let's consider each of those things.

He Became Sin

2 Corinthians 5:21 says, "God made him who had no sin to be sin for us, so that in him we might become the righteousness of God." Jesus, the perfect, holy, spotless Lamb of God, who was himself the righteousness of God, became sin, *our* sin. It is hard to grasp just how astonishing this is. Imagine that you have a beautiful wedding cake. You're at your wedding reception, and it's time to cut the cake with your new bride or groom. Before you, you see that perfect, delicious masterpiece that you paid the greatest baker in your whole state to create for you. And then someone comes and dumps a massive bucket of sewage on it. No, even worse, they toss it into a whole vat of sewage. Would you eat it? No, of course not. It has been horrifically ruined. That's *sort of* what is like for the spotless Lamb of God to "become sin."

But this means the opposite is true of us! Have you ever done something that just made you feel dirty? Do you have any shame at all in your life? The cross is so incredibly powerful. Once you can start to grasp in your imagination what it means that when Christ takes on our worst deeds into his very self, purity becomes filth, then you can also begin to imagine what it means to "become the righteousness of God."

Imagine somehow the complete removal of such filth. In some ways, this was concretized in the healing of the lepers in the gospels. Look at one of the stories.

> 12 While he was in one of the cities, there came a **man full of leprosy**. And when he saw Jesus, he fell on his face and begged him, "Lord, if you will, you can make me clean." 13 And Jesus stretched out his hand and touched him, saying, "**I will; be clean**." And immediately the leprosy left him. 14 And he charged him to tell no one, but "go and show yourself to the priest, and make an offering for your **cleansing**, as Moses commanded, for a proof to them." (Lk 5:12-14 NIV emphasis added)

This is such a powerful story, because it is not only about the healing of a wasting skin disease but about so much more. Lepers in Bible times were the lowest of the low. The religious teachers taught that lepers were cursed by God because their sins were so much more grievous than anyone else's. In fact, all sickness was a tit for tat payback for personal sins committed. Can you imagine if every time something bad happened, you attached it to something you did wrong? Wouldn't that drive you crazy with worry and guilt? You would be grasping all the time, looking for flaws in yourself, pecked and harassed all day by Satan. But I have great news: that's not the way it works.

But in his day, the leper would have believed this, too. He was a literal outcast. He had to ring a bell when he came into town so that everyone could scatter to avoid getting his leprosy and sin on them. No one wanted to be cursed by association. And then Jesus came along. In St. Matthew's gospel, the leper approaches Jesus as he comes down from teaching the great "Sermon on the Mount." Perhaps he'd heard it. Hearing Jesus boldly and lovingly proclaim that "Blessed are the poor in spirit" and "those who mourn," and "the meek" could have had a faith-building effect on him. Something about Jesus made the leper think Jesus might help him. Maybe he had witnessed one of Jesus' healings and it had given him hope. Was he not the poorest of the "poor in spirit?"

He fell on his face in front of Christ, and he begged. "Lord, if you will, you *can*..." This is profound. The leper knew something about Jesus, and that is that Jesus *can*. He is *able*. The leper had an understanding about the ability of Christ. A lot of us have no problem believing in the awesome power of God. There are so many awesome things in creation—the Grand Canyon, black holes, and microbiology—so we know there simply *must* be a God who is even more awesome and who thought of these and spoke them into being.

But He is Willing

But do most people believe that in addition to being *able,* God is *willing?* I don't think they do. In part, because of the fall, most people seem to struggle with an inherent feeling of self-hatred. They are riddled with guilt, even when they didn't do anything. This is sometimes made much worse by caretakers who use this sense of guilt to their advantage to control their children. But even when that is not the case, there is a sense of shame that comes with the doctrine of original sin. David understood this when he said, 5 "Surely I was sinful at birth, sinful from the time my mother conceived me. 6 Yet you desired faithfulness even in the womb..." (Ps 51:5-6a NIV).

The prophet Isaiah understood this when he said, "We all, like sheep, have gone astray, each of us has turned to our own way; and the Lord has laid on him the iniquity of us all" (Isa 53:6).

Paul understood it when he said, "for all have sinned and fall short of the glory of God" (Ro 3:23). And Adam and Eve understood this when they went from being "naked and unashamed," (Gen 2:25) to "I was afraid because I was naked; so I hid" (Gen 3:10b).

Consequently, we don't feel loveable, unless we can somehow earn it. Trying to earn love is a losing battle, because no matter how much we try, we never can get beyond naked, ashamed, and wanting to hide from God. At least not on our own. Add on top of that the leper's supposed *proof* he was cursed, and you can imagine it must have taken a lot for him to approach Jesus. You can also imagine why, although he was sure that Jesus was able, he still had to ask if he was willing.

Right now, I want you to ask yourself if you believe in both the power of God *and* the love of God *for you*. Jesus loves you, not just everyone else! He became sin, so that he could give us his righteousness. He traded places with us, because he loves us. And not only did this absorb God's wrath for our sins, but it made us into new and loveable creations! You can be new. You can be unashamed. And what we will discuss later is that you can be like Christ and learn to emulate his love in so many different ways.

If only you knew what I know about the love of God! My goal is to help you to know, so you can rehearse this great truth. God truly loves you, and he has done everything to prove it!

Abandoned by the Father

In the above section, I said there were two things Jesus feared in the garden of Gethsemane. Besides the horror of the cross, he was to be abandoned by his Father in heaven for the first time in all of eternity.

Psalm 22:1 says, "My God, my God, why have you forsaken me? Why are you so far from saving me, from the words of my groaning?" Originally penned by King David when he was in distress, we remember this verse mostly because the first part of it was quoted by Jesus on the cross.

Some people have been confused by this. Why would Jesus say these words? Didn't he know why he was being "forsaken"? That was the plan, wasn't it? First, I simply want to show that Jesus was abandoned by God in this trial. He was forsaken. This must have needed to happen for him to take our sins and to die. As I said above, I believe this forsaking was what had made Christ so anxious in the garden. He had had a connection with his Father in heaven for eternity. What could be more devastating to Christ than to be forsaken by the Father?

But I don't think he actually didn't know the reason why the Father was forsaking him. Here is a side note: The really cool thing Jesus teaches us here is how to pray with the Psalms. If you feel forsaken, alone, like God even just *might* not be watching, then you can pray back to God his own Word. Praying the Psalms teaches us in the school of prayer how to be honest with God like David was. There is great power in praying back to God his own Word.

Now that I have experienced the presence and love of God, I can understand why the loss of his presence was such a traumatic experience for God the Son. In the next chapter, I want to take some time to tell you what it was like before God revealed himself and his love to me. Maybe you can identify with my experience.

Chapter 2

My Life Before Christ

I am animated every day by the love I know God has for me, but I was not always this way. I grew up on the North Shore, fifteen minutes from Boston in Saugus, MA. I am the youngest of four boys and come from French and Irish Catholic heritage. We were involved in our local parish, St. Margaret's. My mom was the foundation of faith in my family and the main reason I ever went to church. She grew up going to church constantly, even daily during Lent. I was educated at the parish school, and I attended CCD classes (Confraternity of Christian Doctrine) in the homes of people who would do the teaching. I even played CYO basketball for years on the St. Margaret's team.

We went to St. Margaret's all the way through my confirmation and first communion and penance. These traditions in the Catholic Church are ancient, and, until recently, a given for one born into a Catholic family. First, youth are instructed in an understanding of baptism, communion, and reconciliation, along with confession and penance. Last comes confirmation, before graduation from high school. As the youth are taught, they undergo their first experience of these sacraments. They have already been baptized at birth. If they haven't, it was because the family had not been practicing at the time of their birth, and they were baptized after confirmation. Then, after learning about the Eucharist, or the mystery of the Lord's Supper, they receive their first communion.

This is a big deal, a rite of passage that is celebrated by the extended family.

From my understanding, various Protestant traditions have similar rites of passage for their youth. Some churches have a confirmation class to indoctrinate the youth before they take communion. Protestant churches practice infant baptism, while others merely dedicate their children to God and baptize them later when they make a personal profession of faith. Some churches have formal theological training for their young people, while others encourage the parents to "raise up a child in the way he should go" (Pr 22:6), hoping and praying that the rest of the verse, "and when he is old, he will not depart from it," proves true.

Though I did not feel particularly close to God as I was growing up and going through these steps, I know that my upbringing had a positive impact on me. Later, when I would come to know Christ, the foundation for my faith was already laid. Now, as someone who works with youth in the church, I am concerned. The youth of today, at least those in my area of the United States, are really struggling. Back then, most of us were at least somewhat involved with a church that was the center of our community. As I stated above, the Bible says, "Train up a child in the way he should go: and when he is old, he will not depart from it" (Pr 22:6 KJV). As long as the experience is a net positive one, then a strong biblical foundation will come back around when one is grown. Of course, some people's experience growing up in church is not positive. In those cases, a real tragedy has occurred, and the sinfulness of humanity has gotten in the way between the child and his or her God who loves them. Unfortunately, they may never know.

But today, the issue is negligence. The relationship with Christ is not established. We're not teaching our youth, so they have no intimate relationship with Christ as they enter young adulthood. They have no knowledge of prayer. While they may be able to recite certain rote prayers, they are never taught how to pray to God, praise him, or to hear and feel him in their spirit, their mind. Youth today are deprived of the opportunity to bask in his glory after they confess their sins, relinquishing the guilt of their non-Christlike actions. They don't get to learn how to seek forgiveness and guidance from Christ Almighty or worship him for who he is. It is as though they are sent into a vast forest but can only see individual trees, bushes, and entangled weeds. It is the whole of the forest that would show them the love of God, but they only encounter the narrowness of one tree here and another tree there. This drastically minimizes their view of God, until the God they are rejecting is not the God of the universe at all.

I remember when my mother used to make my brothers, Steve, Kevin, Brian, and me go to mass. When she was unable to go, we would go and bring back the bulletin to prove that we had attended. At least, that is what we thought we needed to do. Sometimes, my older brothers would take the bulletin and just leave. I don't remember ever doing that. I would just get a bulletin and sit in a pew until mass was over. We had a very strict priest at St. Margaret's, one that would stop in the middle of the first reading if you came in late. He would stand up and watch and stare at you as you entered the church from the back. He would wait until you proceeded down the aisle, watch you struggle to find a seat, stare intently at you, and keep waiting until you were seated, still staring at you intently as you settled into the pew. Only then would he allow the reader to proceed with the rest of reading. He was calling you out for the entire congregation to bear witness!

I knew that if he figured out what my older brothers were doing, he would certainly tell my mother. As I look back, I see that his actions were quite simple. For Catholics, the grace and glory of our Lord is the

Mass—is the Church—and if one cannot understand that and dedicate themselves to such an amazing event each Sunday morning, the priest felt one should be made aware of their lost dedication! "The first will be last and last will be first in the kingdom of God," but apparently not on this earth, according to our priest at St. Margaret's!

After getting diabetes a lot changed for me with the overwhelming responsibility of taking care of myself so that I would not die an early death and would live a long life. By age twelve, I was practically grown up, and a subtle depression was already taking form. By the time I'd reached my twenties, I had already seen spiritual signals, or markers. Today I can look back and see them clearly, but at those times, they were only a dim image.

I did sometimes communicate with God in prayer. I had no daily prayer routine, but something would always happen to me when people I knew, and especially people I loved, had some kind of trouble. Something would come over me, and I would find myself sobbing and crying out to God to help them. I never told a soul about these times, but most of the time, God seemed to answer my prayers. I would get the answer through him providing what I asked for, or from a symbol of the answer. At very least, he would give me the grace to help. Some might call it coincidence, but in every case, after I prayed, something unbelievable happened. I know I doubted at times, but I also know I was seeing remarkable things take place. I felt God actually heard my cries for help.

It's Not Her Time!

Here is an example of those times. I had two cousins who also were afflicted with type one diabetes. This disease usually runs in families. My grandmother also had it. To me, having diabetes was a struggle, but having a band of family members who shared the struggle was like having a support group. Since there was an age gap between my cousins and me, we did not talk much about it, but mentally, there was a sense of togetherness and a common understanding. It makes a big difference having people in your own family who can understand what you are going through. They did not know this, but I loved them so much more because of our shared plight and anguish. Any diabetic and anyone with a disease or illness will and can understand this.

When I was in my early twenties, one of my diabetic cousins was in serious trouble. She had been admitted to the hospital, and it was not going well. From what my mother explained to me, the prognosis was grim, and I was in total shock. First of all, I loved her. I felt the connection I already described and was probably getting a greater sense of my own mortality seeing her struggle. I felt heartbroken and furious, like a mother lion who has her baby cub taken away. I had such a sense of injustice at the fallen state of a world in which sickness can have its way. For this reason, I always remember having a deep feeling of connection with the reading of Christ's response to Lazarus' death. "Jesus wept."

Darrin wept—which is an understatement. I cried out fiercely. When I heard about the gravity of my cousin's condition, I was driving to work, distraught, and screaming at God all the way down the highway. I yelled at him at the top of my lungs, "No! It is not her time! She has more to do on this earth through your will, Lord! Let her survive and give her a chance to show your grace to others!" I could hardly see the road through my tears as I pounded the steering wheel in indignation at the injustice of the fallen world at seventy-five miles per hour. "She's not done! She's not done!"

I cried, "Save her, Lord! Bring down your grace and glory upon her! Your will needs to flow through her once again. She has more to do!"

I was sobbing, and begging, determined to make him her me. My voice resonated through my head and car like an opera singer over a Wagnerian orchestra across a massive crowd, only greater in magnitude. I wanted all of heaven to hear me.

Completely distraught, I arrived at work and settled down in the parking lot before trying to go in. As the day wore on, something came over me. By late afternoon, I didn't understand it, but I had a strong sense that I needed to go to the hospital. The feeling was overwhelming, running through me like a stream. Work ran late that day, and it was not until 8 p.m. that I was able to get to the hospital, which was in the next town over. I went directly to the nurses' station and heard from the nurse on duty that unfortunately, visiting hours were over. I told her that I just needed to be by my cousin—I just needed to pray for her, by her room or bedside. I begged the nurse for just fifteen minutes. I promised to stay by the doorway and not even enter the room.

She turned away from me and pretended I wasn't there! She couldn't let me break the rules, but what could she do if she didn't see me? I was elated and felt I had "secret access." What an amazing nurse! I'm still thankful for her. The door to my cousin's room was wide open. She was on the bed, wires and tubes connecting her to screens and equipment all around her. Except for the low light from the screens and from the hallway, it was dark in the room, and I couldn't see too well. The light from the hall lit my path amazingly from the door to the foot of her bed, and the way it led me to her comforted me.

I proceeded to pray. I asked God for his guidance, his peace, his glory, and his healing. I asked him to help my dear cousin, my partner in the family diabetes club, to regain her health and strength. I also asked him to forgive her sins and make her holy and righteous through Christ again, knowing that she may have gotten somewhat far from him. Then

I prayed an "Our Father" and a "Hail Mary," and waited a few more minutes before I "snuck" past the nurse and went home.

Answered Prayer

Days later, I heard from my mother that my cousin left the hospital. God does not always heal the sick. It is safe to say that everyone Jesus healed in his earthly ministry eventually died, even those he raised from the dead. But I got an amazing sense that he healed my cousin, and I was amazed. At other times, I've had the very same sense that God was compelling me to pray for someone, and they have not gotten healed.

Father Grant

I always believed in God, and there were times I would see glimpses of him. There was this priest, Father Grant, at our Lady of Assumption in Lynnfield, MA, who was in his seventies. When I was a young man, engaged to be married, his sermons would strike a nerve with me. No matter what he was teaching about in his homilies in Mass, he would always bring it around to death and eternal life with God. When he did this, his words were absorbed into my mind and soul in a complete fullness of acknowledgment. It was absolutely remarkable. I bring this up because even then I knew that Father Grant wasn't just talking about something he had studied or heard about second hand. He was a man who *knew*. Understand me when I say that he wasn't just an effective communicator. He wasn't just arguing a competent case. I wasn't just weighing his statements logically. I was *receiving* his word. My spirit was accepting the truth of what he was saying.

Since those days, I have had many experiences and encounters with the living God, which I will explain in the next chapter. Sitting under the proclamation of life and death and eternity from the mouth of Father Grant was a very similar experience. The word of God was flowing like a raging river through my soul, mind, my whole being. Every word was lodging itself into the fabric of who I am. Sitting in church with Father Grant was the first of many such experiences with God.

Even before my own revelations, I harmonized with Father Grant when he spoke of God and eternal things. When he read the Bible, he was speaking of what he knew. When he spoke of God, he was speaking of an intimate friend. When words of the fullness of truth came out of his mouth, they hit me in the fabric of my being. One way to describe it would be like there was an experience of pleasure-filled Joy in my bones, the joints, the marrow, particularly as he spoke of the love and mercy of God. Hebrews 4:12 says,

> For the word of God is living and active, sharper than any two-edged sword, piercing to the division of soul and of spirit, of joints and of marrow, and discerning the thoughts and intentions of the heart.

This is truly what was happening, though I had no words to explain it. John 7:38-39 says,

> Whoever believes in me, as the Scripture has said, 'Out of his heart will flow rivers of living water.'" Now this he said about the Spirit, whom those who believed in him were to receive, for as yet the Spirit had not been given, because Jesus was not yet glorified.

This was none other than the Holy Spirit flowing through the words of a righteous and Spirit-filled preacher. I understood later that the experience I was having was resonating as a reminder of my childhood diabetic NDAs, though I had not yet learned to identify them for what they were.

It is difficult for some people to talk about death or to listen to someone talk about death and embrace the reality of it. They don't *know*, but I knew Father Grant was speaking the Truth. I found myself not only listening, but listening intently over the next 30 years as I experienced encounter after encounter through priests, speakers, evangelists, and masses. Most of them did not even come close to describing the love of God and the reality of everlasting life, but Father Grant was on a whole different level. He *knew*.

But back then I still had only a nominal faith and was living all wrong. I did not love people in the way God loves me and calls me to love others. I lived for my own will, confused as it was. I lived for myself with no thought of living for God. It didn't even occur to me, and living for myself was getting me nowhere—at least nowhere good.

Thinking back on Father Grant's messages, it's somewhat astonishing to me now that though I believed him, it did not yet cause a huge change in my life. Like I said, I knew he was telling the truth, but hearing the same things now just completely rocks my world, knowing now what I know. It makes it hard to believe that I didn't fall on my knees at his preaching and repent!

I was talking to a friend the other day who had been a professional classical singer. He was saying that after he had converted to Christianity, he was shocked to realize how powerful some of the sacred classical music is that he'd sung for a decade without being moved. Afterwards, he could no longer perform without crying. It takes being reborn in Christ to grasp the spiritual. With my limited amount of faith, I had a limited sense of God. But now, everything has me in awe. St. Paul said:

One with God

9 However, as it is written:

"What no eye has seen,
   what no ear has heard,
and what no human mind has conceived"—
   the things God has prepared for those who love him—
10 these are the things God has revealed to us by his Spirit.

The Spirit searches all things, even the deep things of God. 11 For who knows a person's thoughts except their own spirit within them? In the same way no one knows the thoughts of God except the Spirit of God. 12 What we have received is not the spirit of the world, but the Spirit who is from God, so that we may understand what God has freely given us. 13 This is what we speak, not in words taught us by human wisdom but in words taught by the Spirit, explaining spiritual realities with Spirit-taught words. 14 The person without the Spirit does not accept the things that come from the Spirit of God but considers them foolishness, and cannot understand them because they are discerned only through the Spirit. 15 The person with the Spirit makes judgments about all things, but such a person is not subject to merely human judgments, 16 for,

"Who has known the mind of the Lord so as to instruct him?"
But we have the mind of Christ. (1 Cor 2:9-16 NIV emphasis added)

"No human mind has conceived the things God has prepared for those who love him." This is incredible. In life we go around getting inputs through our senses. There are things to see, smell, touch, hear, and taste. We perceive things, and then we must figure out what to make of them. Paul says this is not just about the eyes and ears. There is a sixth sense that God gives believers to have *spiritual perception.* Paul says here that this is having "the mind of Christ!" These are "spiritual realities."

I am writing this book, because by receiving the words of truth, my hope is that God would open your spiritual eyes. When you can hear of the realities of Heaven and be in awe, then you know you have spiritual perception. When you can see the beauty of God in the things he has created, then you have his Spirit in you giving spiritual eyes. When you can be overcome by the love of God, then you are beginning to know him.

Before my true conversion, something told me Father Grant was speaking the truth, but it didn't really move me yet the way it should have. I was growing, but I was growing by tiny baby steps. I remember when my cousin, Patty, was near death. She was only in her twenties. I know that in my soul I was deeply offended by death. She was too young. I just knew that it was not right that she, or anyone for that matter, should die. Death had been such a constant specter in my life, and I felt hatred toward it. I prayed to God, "Her story is not done! She has more to offer! Please Lord, let her live and continue what she needs to do in her life!" To my amazement, she lived.

Diabetic Episodes

Throughout my childhood, teens, and twenties, I had various diabetic episodes. Especially when I was younger, these were horrific. Some even left me in the hospital. During a typical episode I was unconscious on the floor, lying in a large pool of my sweat, my clothes soaked through, death gurgles emanating from my mouth, and fighting for my life. But even then, despite my body's clinging for life, unconsciously not knowing the state I was in physically, there would be total peace from which I did not want to return. And returning from that place, both then and later, felt like I was passing through hell. I will describe this more in the next chapter.

By the time I was thirty, I had been growing spiritually little by little. I went to church, but not every week. I was married with children. If there are fifty levels of faith, then I had grown from about level one to six. I still had anger. I still experienced a fair amount of dullness. But somehow, getting to this point prepared me for a propulsion of faith that caused me to skip a few levels all at once. Before, I didn't attend church every week and I didn't pray every day. Nowadays, I love church and try to be there whenever the doors are open. I pray without ceasing now, because prayer in the presence of my loving Father is my greatest joy, but I'll describe this in a later chapter. So how did I get to where I am now? Keep reading.

Chapter 3

From Six to Thirty and Encountering God

I was a 30-year-old type one diabetic working long 10-to-12-hour days. This is not a great situation when you are too busy to eat healthily and have to inject insulin four to five times per day. One day I came home from work just like I always did, but I felt extremely exhausted. Any diabetics who are reading this will understand that there are warning signs, "tell-signs," that signal an emergency when blood sugar levels are falling drastically, dangerously low. Your ability to speak is altered, your awareness of the situation becomes a little fuzzy, which makes it hard to think clearly about what is happening so you can make good decisions about what to do.

At 30, getting tired is a sign that something is not right, and I was beyond tired. What complicated the situation was that I was not used to working so much, so I just thought I was exhausted from work—that anyone would be tired from such long hours. Then I did the worst thing you can do in that situation. I went upstairs and lay down in my bed. I should say, it's *normally* the worst thing a diabetic can do. For me, it led to the most amazing and life-altering experience of my existence.

What I am about to reveal was an astonishing and unbelievable blessing.

As I lay in my bed, I fell into a major low blood sugar reaction, my levels dropping below 25. Normal levels are 80-120, so this is alarming. I once dropped to 28 in a restaurant and the paramedics thought their meter was broken, because I was still able to talk to them since I'd already had so many "low" episodes in my life that my body had somewhat accustomed to it and normalized itself in a way to the lower levels. But this day, at 25, I was becoming unconscious, moving in and out of consciousness. I don't remember getting out of bed, but what I remember is that I was outside my bedroom standing at the top of the stairs looking straight at my wife. I was barely conscious and fighting to stay conscious, reaching out for my wife.

As the sugar is becoming more and more depleted, the brain starts shutting down, but when a remnant of sugar reaches a certain area of the body, like sight, or consciousness, I get what I call "still pictures." These images in my brain are like snapshots. I was in a serious low blood sugar reaction and in major trouble.

After the moment I reached my arm out to my wife, everything changed. I do not remember any point after that moment on the outside in terms of what was happening physically with my body. I was no longer looking out of my own eyes. Everything I do remember was happening outside of my physical self. I was suddenly looking down on myself from the corner of the wall and the ceiling of my hallway. My body was down there, standing at the top of the stairs where it had been. This part is extremely important to understand. My body "down there" was still functioning and standing, still reaching out its arm to my wife, at which point, things became unbelievable.

I felt I was in a whirlwind, like a tornado tunnel. I am still out of my body and at a fullness of peace that is unbelievable. There is no hurt, no pain, and there are no worries. I couldn't see myself or my wife anymore, and I could suddenly hear the laughing of many children. It was a soulfully, unimaginably pure laughter. It was pure, innocent, and the most worry-free laughter I have ever heard. It was not only the sound, but the laughter was resonating through me, through my entire soul, bringing me back to the pureness of me, comforted, and worry-free the way I was as a child before I knew of my condition. Reflecting later I was reminded of Scripture, "Truly I say to you, unless you turn and become like children, you will never enter the kingdom of heaven" (Mt 18:3).

Jesus explains that his disciples need to become like innocent children—loving and pure. The disciples had been arguing about which of them was the greatest and should deserve to sit next to Jesus in His kingdom. But God was giving me proof through this amazing experience that Christ's words were true, and he allowed me to experience the purity of a child within my soul so that later I would understand the meaning of Jesus' words. As I write of this experience, the tears well up in my eyes. It was such an unbelievable, amazing, and simple experience with God, the first of many throughout the years.

After the children's' laughter, the love of God filled every fiber of my being, my soul. The moment, as much as I am trying, is indescribable. My field of work is engineering in the medical device manufacturing environment, so I really only know how to describe things quantitatively, but I want you to understand emotionally, soulfully, and spiritually. I want you to somehow understand and comprehend what can be understood from this one statement: *God's love fills my entire soul.*

When God enters into my soul in this way, his love is drowning. When this happened, I could feel God's love all around me and right through me. God became one with me entirely—with me, in me, and encompassing me totally. The size of his love for me is massive, unmeasurable, overwhelming, infinitely large. It is indescribable the amount of love poured into and through me. I am so enriched, intoxicated by it. If I were an empty vase, and then his love was poured into me and overflowed after filling me up like water which is God's love. Again, the simplest way to say it is that my entire soul is filled up when that happens.

What is the purest and simplest love you can imagine? It is as innocent as a child's laughter. You have never felt anything so simple and so pure. The feeling that came over my soul was remarkable. It was like someone came along and gave you the answer to the complex problem you'd been asking forever. Have you ever had that happen? You are trying so hard to solve a complex problem, and when someone gives you the answer, you can't believe how simple it actually is? It's a previously unsolvable mystery suddenly solved! The feeling of God's love entering my soul felt just like that and drew me entirely into his amazing glory and LOVE. I was able to see the Way, the *Life*. I could see how he wanted me to live, the unbelievably simple way he wanted me to love others by the simple way he was extravagantly loving me.

I was conscious in the moment of thinking, "What have I done? I have it all wrong." At that time, I did not know that God was listening to me.

God's pure simplistic love was so encompassing that it led me to think of what he wanted all along. He was showing his massive love by consuming me with it. In the simplest purity he was telling me that I had been doing it all wrong on earth. God's love is so simple and pure, amazingly pure, and all he was telling me with this massive outpouring of love was that he wanted me to love this way, his way, in the pureness of his love for him and for anyone. God had poured himself entirely into my soul and showed me the way through his grace and love. He taught me everything in this way—and I mean *everything*.

My great hope and prayer when you read this is that somehow using mere words you can experience some measure of this. God's love for you is massive—trust me—unbelievably massive. Using the experience and language of this earth, I will try to explain that. The engineer in me wants to express it quantitatively in a measurement exercise that is more understandable. I'd like you to go on a dream walk with me, a thought walk. Find a place that is quiet with no distractions and get your mind to a place of no worries and make sure there will be no interruptions as you bring up a thought or moment in your life.

I want to encourage you to try this: Close your eyes to capture a moment in your mind. Try to remember a time when you were loved. It could be a hug from a boyfriend or girlfriend, mom or dad, or someone special in your life.

It could also be a memory of an experience of tasting something that you haven't had in many years, but now is filtering through your taste buds and what rushes through your head is that glorious chemical rush of tasting something wonderful when you are incredibly hungry. The wonderful taste consumes you and your eyes roll into the back of your head as you remember and savor this taste.

It could also be a sensation of you loving and being with someone intimately. Think of a particular love experience. It's very important to understand the size of that feeling in you on that one moment in your life that you consider to be unbelievably amazing. Maybe it is a type of moment when you felt love within your mind, heart, body, and soul, a moment you have always remembered where you were drowned in that love, warmth throughout your body, bursting with love.

Imagine all these feelings and sensations combined. If you have that in your mind now, and it's radiating through you and in as a visceral and delightful memory, I want you to try to imagine what it would be like to multiply this feeling by a factor of 10,000. Are you thinking this is humanly impossible?

The most glorious feeling of love in your life multiplied by 10,000 doesn't even compare with God's love. Go outside what seems humanly possible for a moment. Try, just try to comprehend what that would be like. It's insane, wouldn't you agree? It's impossible to grasp such an intense feeling—impossible to measure.

Okay, stay with me. I want you now to take the 10,000x multiplier of your most profound love and pleasure moment, and place it individually inside every single, solitary microscopic, cellular molecule in your body. Let me rephrase that.

God is one with you entirely when he enters into your soul, and his love for you is massively intensified to the highest possible level in every molecule. Your entire soul is filled, and filled, and filled again. If you can get there in your mind, I now gracefully welcome you to the LOVE, the PEACE, the GRACE, the GLORY and the ALMIGHTY POWER of GOD.

I am once again bursting into tears as I write and remember these times with my Lord. There is nothing more profound and amazing than this alone. Nothing! I hope this begins to give you an understanding of how much God truly, unconditionally loves you, just you, and you alone. I'm not saying that God doesn't love others, but you must experience this as personal. He wants you to feel some kind of exclusivity with him as he pours the full light of love onto, into, and through you. When God is within you in the fullness of Spirit and soul, there is pure simple, highly concentrated love, pureness of peace, and no worries, cares, pain, issues, or even time. There is unbelievable security that is unreal and amazing.

Think about it! The fact is that God is completely with you in heaven and encompasses you in your soul as he shows you all his love, his peace, and his power. By showing you that he is one with you, he is letting you know he was with you all along. All he has ever wanted you to do is to fill the amazing world with his simple love to the best of your ability. Through my experiences I have found that God was showing me his own amazement and glory. He was inadvertently letting me know he is, was, and always has and will be with me. I did not know it on earth to the fullest I should have and could have. It is *unbelievable*!

Once you have experienced him and are back on earth, you know, and it changes your life. My great hope and prayer is that what I am telling you as I sit here weeping in rapture is helping you in some way to experience something that will change your life. I want to help so much. That's why I'm here.

While in God's glory, encapsulated in the entirety of his love, I was at times able to think and ask questions. I was scared, but still fully engulfed in love. What amazes me as I reflect now, is that as I thought of a question while God was within me entirely, he would answer me. As soon as there was a question in my soul, instantaneously God responded. I mean he responded at the beginning of my question before I could finish asking it, not at the end. I thought, Wow! God within me knows all and speaks all with instantaneous telepathic communication — pure, fine, simplistic instantaneous knowing running through me with answers throughout my soul. God's grace, God's love, his Word was communicating to me within me — my thoughts, questions, and the answers all coming at once. Amazing!

I learned in this way of the massive complexity of God. If you think our bodies, languages, and the cells of our eyeballs are complex, trust me, God is at a level we could never understand. His power is incredible!

When he focuses his love on you it is so complex and simple at the same time. His love is so unconditional, so pure, so massive, it puts the complexity of the human body and the whole universe to shame! There is simply no comparison of any kind. Of all the things he has created, not one of them is so amazing as the thoughts of God and his ability to communicate and be present.

At one point throughout this experience, God started to show me my ways. He showed me not only in a visible sense, but in a soulful and feeling sense. I rapidly could see most of my life experiences. Everything I had said and did with people throughout my life, every episode, every word, every thought and feeling, every reaction of others around me was coming to me all at once. Wow! Imagine the mind of God to focus on all things simultaneously! He was showing me a glimpse of that.

God let me feel everything while staying right with me in the background of my soul in the fulfillment of his love in its entirety. I've heard this referred to as Life Reveal when it is referring to what happens in heaven when we are shown our life. I was getting a foretaste of that experience. As amazing as this was, it was not easy. In my short 30 years of existence to that point, there had been good times and really bad times. Even when I was shown horrible things that I had done, God's love and unconditional acceptance of me did not waiver. If it had, it would have been too much to bear! He truly loved me! God sees it all, hears it all, and knows it all, and he still loves us! Trust me. He knows you in the same way, and he loves you!

This was a huge point of revelation for me, because I knew the very instant that God entered my soul and revealed his unconditional and pure love for me. I had felt this before in other diabetic reactions during my teens and twenties, but I had not recognized it for what it was, the presence of God. I had been consumed in this pure unconditional love in those times. He was holding me in his arms and in the simple purity of his love for me. I just didn't know it, but now I do.

I have seen Christ in his glory. I have seen his face. It was the color and brightness of the sun ten times over and extremely difficult to look at. His robe was a magnificent, shining white. It was the whitest white I had ever seen. It was astonishing. Seeing him that way reminded me that I had seen him that way before this time in past low blood sugar reactions—there in his white robe in massive brightness, I can see the structure of his body. Even now I can see it as I close my eyes. In low blood sugar episodes, I see a massive brightness in an internal mind porthole even as I am slightly conscious and in an extremely dangerous state.

I don't know how I left his presence, but I'm sad to say that I did. People who have these kinds of experiences say they wish they hadn't come back. I feel the same. Once you are with God, you don't want to be anywhere else. There's no comparison to the profound feeling of being in his presence, love, and glory.

I remember the instant I was back in my body in the same place at the top of the stairs, only now I was on a stretcher. When the stretcher was lifted up by the paramedics, I was at once reminded of being lifted up to the rafters just a little bit earlier, which confused me, because I was not totally "with it" yet. I was in somewhat of a trance, I remember it completely, and I was reciting the Our Father (The Lord's Prayer for my Protestant brothers and sisters). I recited it over and over again, the words resonating through me. I was chanting this prayer, and every word filled my soul, every sentence was insanely encapsulated within me. The understanding of each word, each phrase, each sentence in full knowledge of mind, heart, soul, and spirit. I embodied the prayer. Since then, whenever I speak the Our Father, it is totally different than before.

My inflection, tone, and the phrasing of the sentences is completely informed by my experience that night. What a prayer God presented in me on my way back to my body and my senses within my soul and flesh! Thank you, Lord Jesus! After that day, I began to live, and still do to this day, a life of God's presence, full of the knowledge of the love of God in all of us. I have lived for him ever since.

Near Death Experiences

It is understandable that if you have not experienced anything like this, it would be hard to wrap your head around. I've experienced it many times, and I have a hard time getting my head around it. But thousands of people have experienced God during a near death episode.

Most famously in relatively recent years, a boy claimed to go to heaven when he was having an appendectomy and told his parents that he had gone to heaven and come back. Their account, *Heaven is for Real*, became a massive bestseller and blockbuster movie. It also sparked some charlatans who faked a similar story, *The Boy Who Came Back from Heaven*, that also made millions before the boy who claimed to go to heaven while in a coma recanted his story and sued the publisher. He said he told the story to get attention and his father knew it, but exploited him anyway.

Another widely read account came from a neurosurgeon, Eban Alexander. *Proof of Heaven: A Neurosurgeon's Journey into the Afterlife (2012)* when he had gone into a medically induced coma for meningitis. He has been highly criticized, but having formerly been an atheist, he was previously skeptical of NDEs and the accounts of patients seeing bright lights and feeling God's love. After his experience, his insight was that, though he was brain dead for a time, he had a consciousness and experiences that made him a believer in both a human consciousness outside the brain, *and* a wonderful place we go when we die.

Neurologists have disputed Alexander's findings, but the conversation belongs in the mix of evidence for something. Thousands and thousands of people have reported similar experiences.

The Soul Goes First

A friend of mine is acquainted with a hospice chaplain named Philip. Philip has been doing his job of comforting the dying for thirty years. According to my friend, who is also a pastor, Philip says that there have been hundreds of times as he sat with the dying that they acknowledged some experience happening as they go. They see a light, or a loved one, or Christ. They go from mostly unconscious to conscious and seem to be seeing something that only they can see. They start talking to someone. They start weeping and smiling as though something wonderful is happening. Philip was already a believer and an ordained pastor, but he claims his faith goes through the roof at these times and that it is the greatest blessing of the job.

As I grow older, I tend to hear amazing stories of those who have watched from the bedside of loved ones passing. In my NDE I experienced the taking of my soul while my body was still functioning as I watched it from a distance up high. I know that God takes a soul prior to the body dying, and since I have discussed this particular point with a few close friends, stories have emerged to confirm this. A friend of mine witnessed his mom minutes prior to dying. She was coherent and wide eyed one moment, and then the hospital door just creeped open, freaking my friend out. But his mom was whispering words of amazement and happiness. She passed minutes later, he told me, and he was 100% sure that Christ or an angel walked into that room and took his mom away peacefully and gracefully.

Another woman I know lost her father to a disease that was something like leukemia. After battling it for three years and suffering through two bone marrow transplants, Mike took a turn and ended up back in the hospital. One night, he coded, and alarms started going off, drawing an army of doctors and nurses into the room. In his very last coherent moments, the man heard the doctor ask, "Mike, do you want to live?" He must have nodded, because they put tubes down his throat and hooked him to a breathing machine (he'd been having some respiratory issues at that point, probably pneumonia). He had a living will with a "do not resuscitate" feature, but since he had been able to agree, they "plugged him in."

Though his body lived that way for another two weeks until the family had the machines turned off, everyone who witnessed this watched the light go off shortly after he was hooked up to the ventilator. His daughter who described it could not be convinced that his soul didn't leave shortly after they plugged him in.

I believe these stories because this happened to me in my NDE. I know that God takes all of us prior to dying, prior to our last breath. I think it is because he does not want his children to feel death or to feel the last moment. He wants to bring all of us into his Glory with no pain and no frightening experience of death, from one life on earth to ongoing everlasting life with the Lord. That we are eternally One with God is the Lord's promise.

I hope this helps you fully understand what happens to your soul at death and helps you remove some fear of dying when your time comes. I also hope and pray that you know Christ, that your experience will be going further into his glorious presence in bliss, because all souls live forever, but not all souls live in bliss. The hospice chaplain I wrote about earlier, Philip, said that he didn't only see souls that went to heaven, but also the souls of unbelievers going to some sort of fearful torment. He said that some, as they are passing, are suddenly terrified, seeing something horrible. Their last words are, "Please, no!" And "Help me!" This is also faith-building for Philip as we understand that not everyone who dies goes to heaven.

God is Love

God is love, and he has sent his one and only Son to die for our sins. Anyone who calls on the name of the Lord will be saved. God is righteous and he is perfect justice. The good news about that is that he must judge evil. Think of all the things in the world that you hate, the evil things: child trafficking, slavery, abusive authorities, racism, unfairness, pain, suffering, poverty, and the list goes on. Think of the ways people perpetrate evil on the helpless. No one gets away with anything. No one. God is perfection. He is unable to look away from evil and not ultimately to do something about it.

But that means his justice applies to the evil in our own selves. It applies to our own tendency to be dishonest, cruel, cowardly, lustful, selfish, or whatever else we are prone to that is contrary to the nature of God. No one gets away with anything. Well, there is one way. It is over-the-top astonishing and generous of God to make one way in which justice can be fulfilled and we can be saved. That way is Jesus Christ, who was perfect, and took our punishment.

But…

You must accept this free gift if you want to live. If you want God's grace and mercy to apply to you, you must say, "Yes, I want it!" See the next chapter (4) for a more detailed description. This has been an important tangent.

Part 2

Elements of Faith

Chapter 4

Receiving Salvation and Forgiveness

If you are not a diabetic, I'm glad for you. I don't want to think about who I'd be without my experiences with God in my diabetic comas, but God has a different plan for all of us. In the rest of this book, I want to help you understand the fundamentals of robust and life-giving faith, whether or not you ever have an experience like mine. My prayer is that I could capture with words what God has shown me by experience. Because of my experience of his love, I feel an urgent need to communicate that love to others. I'm glad you're reading this, and I'm praying for you.

In chapter one, I explained the gospel as I discussed the love of God. I'll repeat myself here. We know God's love, because he showed us what love is by the sacrifice of his Son Jesus. Love came to earth and took our place on the cross. Allow me to go back further. Until now I have taken for granted that you know why we needed a Savior.

By the way, did you know that Jesus Christ has been the "Lamb slain since the foundation of the world?" In Revelation 13:8 it says incredibly that those who are saved have their names written in "the Book of Life of the Lamb slain from the foundation of the world." How was Jesus Christ "the Lamb slain from the foundation of the world?" It shows how God exists outside and inside time at once. God the Son was always the sacrifice for sins before man even fell. Adam's fall that plunged the earth into darkness was not a surprise to God. He had planned for it from the beginning.

God created all kinds of matter when he created the world. He created all kinds of organic matter as well as inorganic. 99.9 % of the organic matter was created without freewill. What I mean is that single celled organisms do not have free will. Amoebas do not have free will. Going up the ladder of complexity and higher orders, plants do not have free will. If there is anything in them that desire, it is the desire for life that moves them. Therefore, if there is sunlight, there is no choice in the matter, the plant will reach for it. If there are minerals and if there is water, the plant will take exactly what it needs in order to flourish. It is not able to *choose* otherwise, It is not a choosing being.

Animals don't really choose either. They are driven by appetites and "feelings" like fear, or impulse to hunt or reproduce, fight, or run away. Like plants, they will do what they need to do to flourish and will not choose otherwise. But people, God gave a powerful responsibility. He created man in his image and whatever else that means, it means man has a mind and the ability to make choices. God gave man the capacity to abstract and concretize abstractions. But to have the freedom of choice is to have an inherent problem. If you can choose, you can choose wrongly. God knew that at some point, man would do just that. He would miss the mark. He would sin. He would fall.

When the first man and woman disobeyed God's command, they effectively rebelled against the Lordship of their Creator. They exercised their free will to do what they wanted instead of what he wanted. Man, unlike any other creature, comes with the capacity to choose things that are not good for him. Nothing God commands of us is bad for us. Everything he wants for us is good for us in our quest for abundant life on earth and later in heaven. But to be his image-bearers, we had to be given the choice. Adam was given the choice and he failed. But Jesus Christ was always the Lamb of God, who takes away the sins of the world (Jn 1:29).

God said something like this, "Hey Son, hey Spirit, let's make man in our image," (Gen 1:28). Let's give him dominion over the earth. But he'll have to have free will if he is going to exercise dominion in our image as a delegated authority."

This part here is pure fiction, but I can imagine the Son saying, "whoa, that's risky." I can imagine then the Father saying, "I know, that's why you are going to have to give your life to forgive them. When the time is right."

It is incredible to read in Hebrews 11 about all the heroes of the Old Testament. It says that every one of them were saved by faith in Christ, *though Jesus Christ had not been born yet.* In Romans, Paul explains how Abraham was saved by faith in Christ. Abraham did not have the revelation that you and I have. When Abraham lived, Christ was the Lamb slain, *but* he had not manifested as Christ to die on the cross. But the Bible says that when Abraham believed God, it was counted to him as faith, and his faith was counted as belief in Christ, or in other words, as *righteousness*. God called Abraham into a covenant with him, and he told him to leave his father's country and go to the Promised land and that God would make him the father of many nations. Paul says in Romans 4:18-25

> 18 In hope he believed against hope, that he should become the father of many nations, as he had been told, "So shall your offspring be." 19 He did not weaken in faith when he considered his own body, which was as good as dead (since he was about a hundred years old), or when he considered the barrenness of

Sarah's womb. 20 **No unbelief made him waver** concerning the promise of God, but he grew strong in his faith as he gave glory to God, 21 **fully convinced that God was able** to do what he had promised. 22 That is why **his faith was "counted to him as righteousness**." 23 But the words "it was counted to him" were not written for his sake alone, 24 but for ours also. It will be counted to us who believe in him who raised from the dead Jesus our Lord, 25 who was delivered up for our trespasses and raised for our justification. (Emphasis added)

Now look again at 23-24. "It was counted to him" was not "written for [Abraham's] sake alone, but *for ours also*!" He says that if we "believe in him who raised from the dead Jesus our Lord," we will also be reckoned "righteous." Belief is what saves. Works come about because of our beliefs. But don't be confused into the evil trap of thinking you are saved by works. Only God saves. Only faith in Christ and him who raised Christ from the dead. James adds something helpful here.

14 What good is it, my brothers, if someone says he has faith but does not have works? Can that faith save him? 15 If a brother or sister is poorly clothed and lacking in daily food, 16 and one of you says to them, "Go in peace, be warmed and filled," without giving them the things needed for the body, what good is that? 17 So also faith by itself, if it does not have works, is dead.

18 But someone will say, "You have faith and I have works." Show me your faith apart from your works, and I will show you my faith by my works. 19 You believe that God is one; you do well. Even the demons believe—and shudder! 20 Do you want to be shown, you foolish person, that faith apart from works is useless? 21 Was not Abraham our father justified by works when he offered up his son Isaac on the altar? 22 You see that faith was active along with his works, and faith was completed

by his works; 23 and the Scripture was fulfilled that says, "Abraham believed God, and it was counted to him as righteousness"—and he was called a friend of God. 24 You see that a person is justified by works and not by faith alone. 25 And in the same way was not also Rahab the prostitute justified by works when she received the messengers and sent them out by another way? 26 For as the body apart from the spirit is dead, so also faith apart from works is dead. (Ja 2:14-26)

Some theologians in history have argued that James and Paul contradict one another. You Protestants may know that Martin Luther seriously considered leaving out the Book of James from his German translation, because it *seemed* so contrary to salvation by grace alone, or *sola gratia,* as it is put in Latin. But the truth is that it belongs in the canon because it harmonizes just fine. James is discussing a different angle, but Paul has said that Abraham's works *showed* his belief. The belief, the faith, saved him. The works proved it.

Today in some Christian circles there is an emphasis on praying a prayer, as though there is a religious or magical incantation and saying some words will save you. Children may be instructed to recite a prayer, "Jesus, come into my heart." They might even say, "I am a sinner in need of forgiveness." But do words matter if the life and action betrays a *different belief* than the one stated? Contrary to having said the words is some kind of free ticket to heaven, don't we all live by what we actually believe, rather than what we say we believe?

Abraham did not pray a prayer. He did not invite Jesus, the Father, or the Holy Spirit into his heart. He believed God. He acted as if he believed God. So, God knew his faith was real. Look at your life. Look at your actions, your calendar, your check book register (if you don't know what that is, ask your grandparents!). How do you live? What do you do with your time? How do you spend your money? In other words, what do you believe about life and what does it make you do?

If you believe that life is just for having fun, you will spend your time and money seeking pleasure. If you believe life is about what others think of you, you will spend your time and money buying status. But if you believe that Jesus is the Son of God and that he fulfills, you will spend time and money seeking his face and doing his will.

My friend describes "being saved." He had grown up in the church and knew all the facts about God, but he never knew God. He said he was believer (just like everyone else in his small Texas town), but what he believed in was beer, sex, and popularity. But when he was twenty-six he walked into a church and experienced the presence of Jesus and that experience was well-explained by a powerful exposition from the Bible, the Living word of God. He saw Christ and was saved. His response to that was the only possible response if he believed what he now believed. Jesus is real. If he is real, he is the God and Creator of the universe. God the Father, Son, and Spirit are one, and they are real. If God is real, then he must lay down his life to follow and to serve him.

How about you? How much do you believe what you say you believe? If Jesus is worth anything, isn't he worth everything? Do you claim that God is number one, but you actually put him somewhere way down on the list? Really and truly consider this. Maybe you realize, "yeah, nothing about my life would indicate that I believe Jesus is the real and true Creator and sustainer of all."

But he is. And he made you, loves you, and died for you to be made righteous in him. He has a plan for your life. He has a will that he wants you to get to know. He cares about every single aspect of your life. He cares how you wake up in the morning, how you wash your face, brush your teeth, eat your breakfast, kiss your kids, and go to work. He cares about your work and how you go about it. He cares about every one of your relationships. He wants you to abide in him and thrive in your life. He wants you to learn to have intimacy with him. He wants to be with you in your triumphs and failures, the good times and bad. He wants to celebrate with you when you are happy, and he will weep with you when you are sad.

He wants to be your teacher. No Christian is called not to be a disciple. This means a student of Jesus, the Rabbi. He has given so much life-giving instruction about how to live, how to pray, how to love, and how to give. He wants you to experience the joys of walking in fellowship with him. He has so much for you, but you cannot benefit unless you receive what he has to give.

Christ wants our lives, and as our Maker, he deserves to have them. But that is glorious good news, because you could not come up with a better plan for yourself than the one he has for you. God would tell you the same thing he told the prophet Jeremiah to tell the Israelites:

> 11 For I know the plans I have for you, declares the Lord, plans for welfare and not for evil, to give you a future and a hope. 12 Then you will call upon me and come and pray to me, and I will hear you. 13 You will seek me and find me, when you seek me with all your heart. 14 I will be found by you, declares the Lord…(Jer 29:11-14a)

The context here is that the Israelites were facing the consequences of their unbelief. For that is always the root of sin, rebellion, and failure to keep our side of our covenant with God. We are so deceived by our sin into thinking that God has a hard way for us, and that life is about trying to please him enough to let us into heaven, while at the same time trying to get away with having as much fun as possible by avoiding his commands. Friends, that is from Satan!

The Israelites worshiped God in their rituals, but they did not believe in their hearts that he was real and kept his Word. So they were facing exile and discipline. But Jeremiah had a message of hope for them. And in this message, we can see our own message of hope.

Where have you been? Have you been following God as though you know what is good and that he is your good Father and Creator who is worthy of not only our praise and allegiance, but our obedience? His grace for us is so magnificent. The Israelites rebelled over and over and over again, and he says, "I have plans to do you good, for your welfare, to give you a future and a hope." You can take this for yourself. Oh, the plans God has for your future!

How do I know? Because:

> 16 God so loved the world, that he gave his only Son, that whoever believes in him should not perish but have eternal life. 17 For God did not send his Son into the world to condemn the world, but in order that the world might be saved through him. (Jn 3:16)

What greater message of love than to die for someone! Turn your life over to Jesus and see what he will do. Repent of your sin and allow his substitutionary death on the cross to apply to you so that you can not only be saved from punishment in hell, but you can one day go to your Father in heaven where he will throw his arms wide open to you and say, "Come and share in my Joy and happiness!"

Chapter 5

Forgiving and Loving Others

If you have never received the forgiveness of God for your sins, I pray you did it after you read the last chapter. This chapter will make more sense to you if you have. After my experiences with God, especially at thirty when I realized his presence in the midst of my NDE in my diabetic low blood sugar episodes, I overwhelmingly understood that God loved me, and he had forgiven me of my sins. But my challenge came when he began to show me that he desired for me to forgive others as I had been forgiven.

The first reason that we are supposed to forgive is simple. Jesus commanded it. Jesus had been telling his disciples how to confront someone in the church who had sinned against them. He wanted them to forgive, but to first be honest about what they were forgiving for. After he explained the process of confronting, and if necessary, bringing the church in on it, Peter asked him a question about forgiveness:

> 21 Then Peter came up and said to him, "Lord, how often will my brother sin against me, and I forgive him? As many as seven times?" 22 Jesus said to him, "I do not say to you seven times, but seventy-seven times.
>
> 23 "Therefore the kingdom of heaven may be compared to a king who wished to settle accounts with his servants.

24 When he began to settle, one was brought to him who owed him ten thousand talents. 25 And since he could not pay, his master ordered him to be sold, with his wife and children and all that he had, and payment to be made. 26 So the servant fell on his knees, imploring him, 'Have patience with me, and I will pay you everything.' 27 And out of pity for him, the master of that servant released him and forgave him the debt. 28 But when that same servant went out, he found one of his fellow servants who owed him a hundred denarii, and seizing him, he began to choke him, saying, 'Pay what you owe.' 29 So his fellow servant fell down and pleaded with him, 'Have patience with me, and I will pay you.' 30 He refused and went and put him in prison until he should pay the debt. 31 When his fellow servants saw what had taken place, they were greatly distressed, and they went and reported to their master all that had taken place. 32 Then his master summoned him and said to him, 'You wicked servant! I forgave you all that debt because you pleaded with me. 33 And should not you have had mercy on your fellow servant, as I had mercy on you?' 34 And in anger his master delivered him to the jailers, until he should pay all his debt. 35 So also my heavenly Father will do to every one of you, if you do not forgive your brother from your heart." (Mt 18:21-35)

Don't you love how generous Peter thought he was being when he suggested forgiving up to seven times? Jesus, using hyperbole, may as well have said, "a million times infinity!" He was explaining to them that forgiveness was not a finite resource. If vengeance belongs to the Lord (Ro 12:19), then the freedom from anger and bitterness is a gift from God that never stops giving, *no matter how egregious the sin against you.* Trust me. If they do not repent, then they have much worse than what you could do to them in your unforgiveness coming to them. It is God they need to worry about. You and I are like that kid whose dad is the toughest dad in the neighborhood.

Jesus said that it was like a king who went to collect debts from his servants. When he found out that one of them owed him 10,000 talents, he demanded repayment. The man didn't have the money, and, as was the custom, the king declared that he and his wife and kids would be sold to pay the debt. What did the servant do? He begged for forgiveness. The king was merciful and forgave him the huge debt, setting the man and his family free from slavery. This alone would have been an amazing story that illustrates how God loves to forgive us. It shows that we owe him a great debt and he has done whatever it takes to set us free, not only from the bondage of sin, but from the righteous wrath of God for our sin.

But the story goes on. That same man, forgiven and set free comes across a man who owed him much less than the debt for which he had just been forgiven. Failing to display the same generosity of spirit, the man put him in prison until he could pay his debt. When the king's servants heard of it they reported it back to the king, who called him "wicked servant," for failing to show the mercy that he was shown.

Why did Jesus tell this story? Because wanted his disciples to understand the foundation on which we forgive others. It is because we have been forgiven that we are to act like our Father in heaven to forgive others. When Jesus taught his disciples to pray he taught them to ask the Lord to "forgive us our trespasses as we forgive those who have trespassed against us". Jesus' point seems to be that if we are unable to forgive others, then we have yet to realize that we had much to be forgiven for. If we don't understand God's forgiveness for us, then we are not likely to be able to forgive when we are wronged.

But Forgiveness is Painful

Many people struggle to forgive because, depending on how badly they have been wronged, it is painful to forgive. It feels like it costs us something. It can feel like we are letting someone get away with hurting us. It can feel like an injustice. The fact is that Jesus showed us exactly what this looks like to do this and exactly how painful it can be to forgive. Jesus was on his throne in heaven, one with the Father and the Holy Spirit in loving communion. Then, for the sake of the world, he,

> 6…though he was in the form of God, did not count equality with God a thing to be grasped, 7 but emptied himself, by taking the form of a servant, being born in the likeness of men. 8 And being found in human form, he humbled himself by becoming obedient to the point of death, even death on a cross.

Isn't that alone amazing? How wonderful, merciful, and gracious is our Lord Jesus that he would do that? And why? Because he desired to pay for our rebellion towards him. He came in the most humble way and how did humanity repay him? By rejecting him and murdering him. No matter, because as it turned out, that was the plan all along. He wasn't the "Lamb slain since the foundation of the world" for nothing. Jesus was nailed violently to the cross after being betrayed and denied by some of his closest friends. And what did he say while he was stretched out dying in agony?
"Father forgive them, they know not what they do" (Lk 23:34).

Corrie Ten Boom

You might wonder if that kind of forgiveness is only for Christ to manage. But remember, He expected his disciples to forgive like that too. There have been Christians in history who, though they didn't die to forgive the whole world, they did die to their own bitterness and righteous anger toward others in order to obey Jesus and forgive. One such story of heroic forgiveness can be found in history after a Dutch woman was finally released as one of the only survivors of her family of a Nazi concentration camp. Her name was Corrie Ten Boom. Her story is found in one of her books, *The Hiding Place.*

Corrie's father, Caspar was a watchmaker and jeweler who owned a shop in the Netherlands. The Ten Boom family loved God and so they spent much of their time helping the poor and spreading the love of Christ. When the Nazis invaded their city, they turned their efforts to hiding Jews and helping them escape the Holocaust. They were successful in this for a while, until one day, they were caught. They built a secret room in their home, "the hiding place," where they could hide and care for Jewish people. Estimates are that the Ten Booms helped around 800 Jews escape before they were caught by the Gestapo.

A Dutch informant had tipped off the Gestapo and they raided the Ten Boom home. Because of the well-hidden secret room, none of the six Jews who were hiding there were caught, but the whole Ten Boom family and several friends were rounded up, about thirty-five people, and taken to prison. After a few days, Corrie, her sister Betsie, and their father were taken to concentration camps. Caspar was dead after ten days of the brutal treatment by the Nazis. Betsie also died, but Corrie, thanks to a bookkeep error, was finally released after quite a long time.

Corrie Ten Boom went on to have a fruitful ministry. She was a powerful preacher and evangelist and found herself in Germany, speaking to churches and Christian societies. One night, as she was speaking to a large crowd of Germans about forgiveness, something unexpected occurred. In her words:

It was in a church in Munich that I saw him, a balding heavyset man in a gray overcoat, a brown felt hat clutched between his hands. People were filing out of the basement room where I had just spoken, moving along the rows of wooden chairs to the door at the rear.

It was 1947 and I had come from Holland to defeated Germany with the message that God forgives. ...

And that's when I saw him, working his way forward against the others. One moment I saw the overcoat and the brown hat; the next, a blue uniform and a visored cap with its skull and crossbones.

It came back with a rush: the huge room with its harsh overhead lights, the pathetic pile of dresses and shoes in the center of the floor, the shame of walking naked past this man. I could see my sister's frail form ahead of me, ribs sharp beneath the parchment skin. Betsie, how thin you were!

Betsie and I had been arrested for concealing Jews in our home during the Nazi occupation of Holland; this man had been a guard at Ravensbrück concentration camp where we were sent. ...

"You mentioned Ravensbrück in your talk," he was saying. "I was a guard in there." No, he did not remember me.

"But since that time," he went on, "I have become a Christian. I know that God has forgiven me for the cruel things I did there, but I would like to hear it from your lips as well. Fräulein – "again the hand came out "– will you forgive me?"

One with God

And I stood there—I whose sins had every day to be forgiven—and could not. Betsie had died in that place—could he erase her slow terrible death simply for the asking?

It could not have been many seconds that he stood there, hand held out, but to me it seemed hours as I wrestled with the most difficult thing I had ever had to do.

For I had to do it–I knew that. The message that God forgives has a prior condition: that we forgive those who have injured us. "If you do not forgive men their trespasses," Jesus says, "neither will your Father in heaven forgive your trespasses."

I knew it not only as a commandment of God, but as a daily experience. Since the end of the war I had had a home in Holland for victims of Nazi brutality.

Those who were able to forgive their former enemies were able also to return to the outside world and rebuild their lives, no matter what the physical scars. Those who nursed their bitterness remained invalids. It was as simple and as horrible as that.

And still I stood there with the coldness clutching my heart. But forgiveness is not an emotion–I knew that too. Forgiveness is an act of the will, and the will can function regardless of the temperature of the heart.

"Jesus, help me!" I prayed silently. "I can lift my hand. I can do that much. You supply the feeling."

And so woodenly, mechanically, I thrust my hand into the one stretched out to me. And as I did, an incredible thing took place.

The current started in my shoulder, raced down my arm, sprang into our joined hands. And then this healing warmth seemed to flood my whole being, bringing tears to my eyes.

"I forgive you, brother!" I cried. "With all my heart!"

For a long moment we grasped each other's hands, the former guard, and the former prisoner. I had never known God's love so intensely as I did then. (*The Hiding Place*).

Aside from "Father forgive them" from the cross, it's hard to imagine a more powerful moment of forgiveness. The Bible gives us another one though. You might wonder if Jesus could give someone the power to forgive those who are killing them, *as they are killing them,* like he was able to. We have an example of that very thing in Acts 7. After a young evangelist named Stephen is arrested, he gives a power lesson to the Jewish authorities about the redemptive history of Israel, and really the world. Look at what happens as he closes out his sermon/defense:

> 51 "You stiff-necked and uncircumcised in heart and ears! You always resist the Holy Spirit; as your fathers did, so do you. 52 Which of the prophets did your fathers not persecute? And they killed those who foretold the coming of the Just One, of whom you now have become the betrayers and murderers, 53 who have received the law by the direction of angels and have not kept it."
>
> 54 When they heard these things they were cut to the heart, and they gnashed at him with their teeth. 55 But he, being full of the Holy Spirit, gazed into heaven and saw the glory of God, and Jesus standing at the right hand of God, 56 and said, "Look! I see the heavens opened and the Son of Man standing at the right hand of God!"

> 57 Then they cried out with a loud voice, stopped their ears, and ran at him with one accord; 58 and they cast him out of the city and stoned him. And the witnesses laid down their clothes at the feet of a young man named Saul. 59 And they stoned Stephen as he was calling on God and saying, "Lord Jesus, receive my spirit." 60 Then he knelt down and cried out with a loud voice, "**Lord, do not charge them with this sin.**" And when he had said this, he fell asleep. (Acts 7:51-60, NKJV, emphasis added)

Notice in both of these stories how the power of God was present to empower the forgiveness. Forgiveness of this kind is supernatural. It seems that Stephen had been given God's power before he forgave. But Ten Boom seemed to receive it *after* making the choice to forgive. Choosing to forgive will activate God's power to help you release bitterness, anger, and vengeance. God promises that vengeance is his (Ro 12:19). We are not built to be the Judge of all Mankind. God wants us to leave him with that great burden. We are allowed to walk around in freedom. This is part of what it means to respond to Jesus' call:

> 28 Come to Me, all you who labor and are heavy laden, and I will give you rest. 29 Take My yoke upon you and learn from Me, for I am gentle and lowly in heart, and you will find rest for your souls. 30 For My yoke is easy and My burden is light." (Mt 11:28-30 NKJV)

It seems then, that if you don't believe you have it in you to forgive, you can make the hard choice to simply obey. If you are experiencing bitterness and unforgiveness today as you read this, then hear Jesus' words to you. He says "Come to me." The way to do that in this moment is to reach out the hand of forgiveness. Make the choice to say, "I forgive you," and trust that Christ picks up that heavy burden, like a father effortlessly taking a load off his little boy when he is struggling to carry it.

I know the weight of that bitterness. I carried it for a long time. But now, I carry nothing. God has taken my bitterness as he has taken my own sin and shame at the cross. Forgiveness, to me, is simple. **Forgiveness is Love**. Trying to understand *how* to give sometimes is difficult, especially when you are living for yourself alone, going your own way, toward your desires, your wants, seeking your control. That way makes it difficult to forgive when someone has stepped in *your* way.

But to look to Christ, who gave his life for all, is pure love. Christ removed all evil from us and forgave us all our sins by virtue of his death on the cross. It is pure, painful, simple, love. Love. I have found over many years that to forgive someone who has done you a terrible wrong is a great struggle. When someone has committed a horrific act against you, or a loved one, it is hard to forgive. Christ tells us to love our neighbor and even our enemies. But what do we do when our neighbor hasn't loved us, but has done us harm. And what of our enemies? They wouldn't even be our enemies if their very existence didn't hurt somewhat.

I grew up in a slightly dysfunctional home. My father was an alcoholic, and it is hard for anyone who grows up in such an environment to escape picking up some poor life habits and behaviors. I was married to a dear friend at age thirty, but the marriage did not last long. Both of us came to the marriage full of brokenness of which we were unaware. Just prior to getting married, I sought out a therapist for some slight depression that I had attributed to my diabetes and the low blood sugar that accompanies the condition.

But soon enough my sessions led into my childhood and upbringing, and these sessions evolved into ACOA sessions, that is, Adult Children of Alcoholics sessions. From there I began to start the process of breaking the cycle that I did not realize I was in. I just knew I was getting married and needed help to become a loving husband and dad. It would be an understatement to say that therapy was difficult. Gut-wrenching is more accurate. It's more than hard to relive a tough childhood and process extremely difficult times. It was good though. The therapy was completely focused on the trauma of my inner child and learning to love that child that was. The therapy was a good start, but the process of love and healing would not become complete until experiencing the Love of the Father in my NDEs. Alas, the healing for me came too late to prevent my first marriage from ending in divorce.

Prayer for Forgiveness

I have learned about forgiveness from Christ in prayer. As I process my daily sin with him each and every day, considering evil in my heart and all wrong actions, I ask him to show me things. I ask him why; I ask what or how I could have done things differently. I address those comments I made which were hurtful to others. I do this day in and day out. We're all broken, but Christ is the way, the truth, and the life. Before I can forgive others, I must receive forgiveness from Christ.

The forgiveness in Christ is amazing. Prayer is an underrated gift from God, as is the enlightenment that comes with it. But what is most special to me is the knowledge of God. When one sows a thought or feeling in prayer, one reaps a word from Christ, or even a whole sentence or a deed from him. Then, to sow an action, a deed, prayerfully in Christ, one reaps a character. When one does this continually, the action of Christ becomes one's own actions. His thoughts become your thoughts, his ways become your ways, and his heart becomes your heart. This happens by his grace and his glory, and then your deeds get folded into "thy will be done on earth as it is in heaven."

As you help others day in and day out, you begin to understand the needs of others in the very moment of yesterday, today, and tomorrow. I say all this to say that forgiveness is an action of Christ. When others have committed injustice toward you, go to Christ in prayer and his heart to forgive will become your heart. He will reveal to you their issues, problems, the motivations behind their actions, their brokenness, their misery. You will understand with Jesus that "they know not what they do."

This revelation from Christ comes to me, it influences me with and in his LOVE, and his LOVE for me becomes his LOVE through me. You and I were created to be vessels of God. When we yield, that is what we become. You can no more withhold forgiveness, than you could without milk to a baby. In this way, as Christ has loved and forgiven me, then enveloped me with his Spirit and his love, I have been able to forgive many family, friends, strangers, and even my own dad.

I feel beyond blessed to know what I know about this—to know how Christ will love and forgive anyone through me if I yield to his Spirit and his Word of revelation. My sincere hope is that I can both elucidate on this topic for you, *and* inspire you to pray in the same way, giving him all control of your life, heart, and will.

As I learned through the years to be connected through Christ, from my NDEs, and then from my daily experiences in prayer, I learned that my dad was forgiven by God, just like I was. I knew it, and I know that he knows it now since he is with God. He knows that I know he is forgiven by me as well. I knew it down in the deepest places of my heart. In my heart I have forgiven him completely and I believe he is aware of that in fullness with the Lord. But I also believe and feel that he wants to confess to me his sins against me. I think he *needs* to do that in a cathartic, returning prodigal son moment, only in reverse as the prodigal dad when we meet again.

I cannot wait for that moment because I will be so happy for him. It is the purest love in heaven, and he will be finally free. I should know he is with Jesus now in heaven, so there is no question of him *not* being free, but I still believe there will be something powerful for him in being able to do in heaven what he was not able to do on earth, confess to me and seek forgiveness. I know how powerful and life-giving it is to do that, and I want it for him.

You need Christ in forgiveness. You need intimacy with God and his love in order to forgive. Where I find that daily is in prayer, then through symbols, through others, through nature, and even through the presence of angels. Life is just not the same for me anymore since my first experiences with God. I see him everywhere. It is crazy, amazing, and hard to believe, but true!

I know I have forgiven many people over the last thirty years since my first experience of God, and many of them are not even aware. Know that when your situation with someone involves hate, anguish, and pain, that person is not themself. Step away and realize this in the moment. Disconnect yourself and see that they aren't in Christ, but in their own flesh and desires, wants, and even needs. Knowing this is half the battle. It's not personal.

The other half of the battle is giving grace and love for that person. The ultimate step of "love thine enemy," is to pray for them. Become one with Christ in prayer, and his forgiveness will permeate your spirit. We can sympathize with those who are in their own will in life. They make everything about them. This is a hard situation, because it is both selfish and excruciating. They think in that state that they are the only ones who are important. They want to control others and each and every moment with them. They want every day, week, month, and year to be entirely about them, and they are willing to hurt anyone who gets in the way of what they have to have. They will win, even if it means that others will lose.

Let's consider this a little more carefully, because aside from simply knowing and loving God, there is little that is more important than understanding the mind and heart of the "sinner" that hurts you. Day in and day out that need to win and achieve at the expense of others is relentless and never leaves as they continuously hurt those around them. In that state, our will is like the wind. It shifts back and forth, and up and down, going nowhere, but hurting others as it goes.

It is a vicious cycle in its nature, damaging the mind and spirit of itself and others. Eventually, living this way will lead one into isolation with no one willing to be around them. Now, when I encounter a person who is this way, they receive my deepest sympathy. In the moment as I stand before them, taking in the misery and pain they are attempting to inflict on me, I go into deep prayer, of course without their knowledge, and I settle myself in Christ. I disconnect from the hatred, and in my spirit I ask God to forgive them, sometimes right then and sometimes later in the day. I know they are truly lost and "know not what they do."

Again, in prayer it is essential to connect with God, to hear or feel a thought, word, action or deed. It is essential to be in that state of knowing and understanding that your own sins, though they are many, are forgiven, removed from you in fact, and placed on the cross with our Lord. This is to be enlightened in the most powerful and life-giving way. Then it is a privilege to ask Christ to fill you with his glory and righteousness in your prayer.

This cannot be understated: *Your days will be changed forever when you yield to God to live this way.* You will see things in a whole new way. You will have your mind and heart open to eternal reality. Remember what Paul said?

> From now on, therefore, we regard no one according to the flesh. Even though we once regarded Christ according to the flesh, we regard him thus no longer. (2 Cor 5:16)

To regard someone according to the flesh is to see them in a purely human way. But in Christ we are given spiritual eyes to see what God sees. You will know immediately who has Christ in them. You will just know. You will see it in their eyes, their gestures, and you will hear it in their voice. God amazingly shows you the way throughout your day. I call it *putting on the glasses of Christ* and seeing things differently, witnessing the wonderful glory of Christ in the midst of the day to day.

Recently, my wife Shannon and I were shopping at BJ's Wholesale Club. We began walking up to the register to pay for our food, and the lane was nearly wide open. There was only one customer at the register, and she was paying and about to leave. Another man had the same plan and was converging on the lane from another angle. I noticed this, stopped, met his eyes with a smile, and signaled pleasantly that he should go ahead of us.

In the moment, I had no cares or worries. I was content. Though I had not tried to be in Christ, I was in Christ. I felt him and his love. My spirit was on fire, and I felt I must be glowing. The man looked at me, stopped in his tracks, and came over to me. He said, "You have been with Christ, and he is with you now."

Wow! I responded to this stranger with the words, "Blessed are you, for you have not seen, but truly believe." It was such an unbelievable encounter. I was awestruck afterwards. Perhaps I had just witnessed an angel from God. The shocking experience felt like that anyway, like an embrace from God, and the joy in me was overflowing as I just stood there in line with him at the register. The paraphrases of God's Word in Scripture were flowing through me as we stood there talking to each other and aside from my NDEs I have never experienced anything so remarkable. Trust me when I say that God is within you, even when you don't know it.

Back to forgiveness. For me, forgiveness was not always so simple. When I was younger, resentment, anger, and frustration were all part of my being. I would dwell on things for a good while until I realized that the anguish and frustration it caused me wasn't worth it. It was not until after my experiences of God's love that I truly started to change. Knowing his love, and learning to seek it in daily walking, made forgiveness an afterthought. How could I be bitter when I know God? How could I have anger, when I understand my destiny in bliss? How can I withhold forgiveness when Jesus has not only forgiven me, but he has shown his forgiveness for me by his unbelievable, radical, lavish, and loving acceptance of me as I walk daily in his loving presence.

Because of the experience of pure, unadulterated, concentrated bliss, I have no way to hold a grudge. I just don't. Because the floodgates of understanding have been opened to me, I cannot see a person who had committed evil against me as an enemy. I just see someone who is broken, hurt, and miserable, in need of compassion. Because I have seen the goodness of God, I can trust the extreme perfection of his justice. The poor person who has hurt me, may very well suffer hell. To imagine that they will never experience God in the way that I have, is such a tragedy to me. For all I know, the terrors of hell are as extreme as the bliss of heaven.

If you can know by experience or by faith what I know, you can understand the simplicity of forgiveness and love. Simply put God loves us, and he calls us to love others. Jesus would not have said, "love your enemies," as though it was the simplest thing in the world unless it was the simplest thing in the world. Don't look at it as a hard command to obey. Look at it for what it actually is, *permission*. It is permission to leave judgment and vengeance to God. No one gets away with anything. They either turn to God or they pay for all their sins. It does not change one thing if you release them from your bitterness and hatred. But it changes you immensely. It will set you free. Freedom is bliss.

Forgiveness as the Answer to Global Problems

Nelson Mandela is hailed as a great man for many reasons. One of the most amazing reasons is that he was able to prevent the bloodbath that was expected upon the lifting of apartheid in South Africa after he himself languished for almost 20 years in prison on Robin Island. He eventually was released and then overwhelmingly elected the first black President of South Africa, which was made possible by the sad fact that it was the first time in their history that blacks were allowed to vote. Here was now a black president, and a massive black majority who had only just thrown off the chains of oppression. Understandably, many wanted to exact terrible revenge.

If you've never studied South African history, you may not understand just how severely oppressed the blacks were. From 1948 to 1994, the Dutch white minority ruled over the black majority with an iron fist. Blacks were not allowed in Cape Town, and were relegated to the much poorer conditions of places like Soweto, where life expectancy was low, and conditions were miserable. Blacks were trained only to enter the working class, and education was severely limited. In black schools they studied one Shakespearian play, Julius Caesar, because it taught a message of warning to conspirators against the government. They would be considered terrorists and punished severely.

In 1960, 7000 people gathered in Sharpeville to protest the Pass Laws, laws that regulated where blacks could and could not go, and police were instructed to open fire on the protestors, murdering 69 people in cold blood. To get an idea, of what it was like for blacks in those days, what follows is a story written by one of them that illustrates it vividly.

> Last month [very early] on a Wednesday morning . . . there was a loud knock, that rattled the dishes in the cupboard . . . at the front door of Vusi's home. . . . [H]e realized that it was the unmistakable knock of the police that had jolted him from sleep. While he reached for his trousers on the small bench near the bed, he tried to remember what he had done wrong. 'A guy's mere existence is a crime in this cursed world. You break the law without being aware of it, no matter how you try not to,' he thought.
>
> Vusi's mother appeared from behind a tattered curtain which was meant to give a little privacy to her bedroom. All seventy-five years of her, woken up unceremoniously at ungodly hours. 'Hawu, my children, what has made you pay us a visit at this early hour?' she asked slowly, in the manner of the ancient.
>
> The dignity of old age overcame some of the visitors' braggadocio. 'It is abakhulu [white men] who have sent us, magogo [grandmother]. Are you the registered tenant of this house?'

One with God

The old woman nodded.

'It's you that's wanted then. Come with us to the office.'

'Is it trouble, my children?'

'We don't know. Our duty was just to bring the owner of the house in.' . . .

At last she was sitting on the bench before one of the superintendents, a middle-aged man with a beaky nose, thin down-turned lips, a pale pinkish, leathery, veined complexion and impersonal grey eyes. . . .

'Ja, ouma. Wat kan ek doen vir jou?'

Mrs. Nyembezi tried her best to comprehend what was said.

'Jong! You can't even speak Afrikaans?' the white man went on. . . . 'Why don't you pay rent, jong?' And the clerk translated.

'But . . . but, my child, I pay. I've never missed paying. We'd rather go with empty stomachs at home than fail to pay. And I keep all the receipts.' . . .

'You want to say I'm lying ouma? It says here you are in arrears to the amount of one hundred rand with your rent, maan! . . . I want that money paid as quickly as possible. Otherwise you go back to the Bantustan you came from, and your son gets a room in a hostel' [a bleak dormitory for single African men] . . .

'Thank you very much, nkosi. We'll raise the money and pay.' It was like saying she would get a duck and make it lay eggs of gold for her.

* * *

Someone had told [Vusi's sister] that what was happening to them was what had happened to her[:] . . . A person with money goes to the superintendents and tells them that he needs a house badly. [The superintendent asks for a bribe to get the man a house, then asks the man,] 'How much can you afford?'

'Three hundred,' answers the prospective buyer, the thought of what would happen to those who lived in the house never having entered the minds of both men.

'You have a house.'

* * *

[Vusi and his mother were ordered to return to the superintendent's office. A]s soon as he and his mother came . . . all hell broke loose. They were told in the crudest terms that . . . the board had no choice but to repossess its house and give it to another person . . .

They were now homeless.

[When they arrived at their home to pack their belongings,] Beak Nose and Lion Face [two white men] . . . arrived in the van. There were three black men in overalls with them. . . . Beak

Nose and Lion Face barged into the house without knocking. There was no need to knock. . . .

They got to work like mules and soon everything down to the last rag was in the street. When they finished, Beak Nose demanded the keys, and the house was locked. The officials got into the front of the van and the three black men behind. With screeching tires they were gone from sight.

The people, who had all along watched from a distance, converged upon Vusi's mother to ask what was wrong although they had already guessed. They came with shawls draped over their shoulders as if someone had died and they were joining the bereaved in mourning. They did the only thing they could to show that they were grieved at losing a long-time neighbor that way. They collected fifteen rand [a few dollars] . . . https://www.facinghistory.org/confronting-apartheid/chapter-2/experiencing-apartheid)

This is a perfect illustration of what it was like for blacks in Apartheid South Africa, there are much, much worse stories than that. Can you imagine how you would feel under that sort of oppression for so many generations? Can you imagine the vengeance you'd feel in your heart for white South Africans?

Apartheid was lifted, and what whites had always feared was coming true. Blacks in South Africa made up 70-80% of the population. If there were going to be free and fair elections, then blacks would soon take over the country, and that is exactly what happened in 1994, when the racially mixed new parliament elected Nelson Mandela as the first black President. Millions wanted blood to avenge the years of oppression. Only one man stood in the way of the bloodbath that was sure to come.

Nelson Mandela

The day Mandela died; the Chicago Tribune had this to say.

> It was Feb. 11, 1990, when Mandela walked out of prison after almost three full decades.
>
> He was a black man, a revolutionary who once preached armed violence on behalf of the African National Congress. He'd been jailed by a white apartheid government. And many were thinking this was finally their time of revenge.
>
> Who would have been surprised? The blacks of South Africa wouldn't have been the first oppressed group to grab the knives and cut their former masters down. And the arithmetic for the inevitable reckoning was right there before him.
>
> All he had to do was raise his fist in rage, give an angry series of speeches, manufacture an incident to spark things up and South Africa would have descended into the kind of blood and horror that still plagues some of her neighbors.
>
> South Africa could have gone that route. But Mandela didn't make that angry speech. He didn't raise that clenched fist. He didn't unleash revenge against the whites who had victimized the blacks. Instead he preached tolerance and reconciliation. And so, his nation was spared.
>
> Is it a perfect place? Of course not. South Africa had troubles then and it has troubles now. But it could have been so, so much worse.

Since the news broke that Mandela died, I've read a lot of wise sayings attributed to him. The one that pierced me most was:

"Resentment is like drinking poison and waiting for it to kill your enemy."

Writing about the day he left prison, he recalled, "As I finally walked through those gates ... I felt even at the age of 71 that my life was beginning anew. My 10,000 days of imprisonment were at last over." https://www.chicagotribune.com/news/ct-xpm-2013-12-06-ct-kass-met-1206-20131206-story.html

What was even more remarkable was what Mandela's government chose to do in order to repair some of the damages and heal some of the national wounds. Mandela appointed the Truth and Reconciliation Commission (TRC) to try to reconcile the horrors of the past. No, he did not want the black South Africans to exact revenge, but he knew they had to do something concrete to resolve some of their issues. Archbishop Desmond Tutu of the Anglican Church was the chairman of the TRC, and their mission was to bring about reconciliation.

The process wasn't perfect, and there are still bugs to work out regarding how to implement such a program, but thousands of people participated, and it gave South Africa the chance to begin to repair damage and give some accountability for human rights crimes. To simplify, someone accused of war crimes or of committing injustice against someone of another people group within S. Africa could apply for amnesty, but that had to allow themselves to be confronted by those who they committed crimes against or by their family members if they were dead. They had to be completely forthright and own up to what they had done in a courtroom across from the victims. The victims were then able in most case to pronounce forgiveness. They received the just satisfaction hearing the confession and having the injustice acknowledged to the world, and also the perpetrator was able to grapple with just how destructive his action had been and to whom.

This is powerful, because it is exactly what repentance and forgiveness is meant to accomplish. When you confess your sins, you don't gloss over them. If they were bad, you say they were bad. The one hearing the confession doesn't minimize and say, "Oh, that's nothing," but rather, they hear it for what it is, acknowledge the sin, and pronounce forgiveness. The confessor can then leave the booth knowing that someone knows and has spoken God's forgiveness. It's right and good, and even technically enough, for us to confess our sins to God alone. But God knows that you will often still feel the guilt, because a part of you doesn't know if God can really forgive you for it. That's why the Bible says in Colossians that we are to be, "forgiving each other," and it says, "as the Lord has forgiven you, so you also must forgive" (Col 3:13).

Finally, this book is about the love of God that I first experienced during my diabetic NDE. So, I want to make this clear that forgiveness comes about easiest when we can think of it in the light of God's love for us. He loved us so much that he forgave us. When he asks us to forgive, he is asking us to pay that love forward to others as a sign that we have received his love and forgiveness in our own hearts. This is at the heart of what Jesus meant when he said that if we do not forgive, we will not be forgiven. Another way to put it is, *if we will not forgive, then we have not experienced the freedom and power of forgiveness ourselves.*

If you have been withholding forgiveness, let go of your bitterness and let God be the judge. He is a just God, and he will always do right on earth and at the judgment. You don't need to be God or do his job. It's a huge blessing, a great grace that he wants to take our bitterness and vengeance from us and set us free to love and forgive. If it's hard, go to him and ask him to help you receive his forgiveness for your sins, and *then* ask him to give you the grace to forgive others.

Chapter 6

Prayer

Intercession

My friend says that I have the gift of intercession. Intercessory prayer is prayer for others. To intercede is to go to God on behalf of others. When I hear of something happening to someone, it moves me and drives me to pray. I suppose it is unusual, but I can't do any otherwise. I do want God to help people and I feel compassion when I hear of what is going on, but the true motive for me is intimacy with God. You have to understand it is such a privilege to join God in his work.

My wife Shannon's father, we call him Papa, drove a minivan each day taking kids to school who had special needs. One day when they were short staffed, he was asked to help out on another run to pick up some kids up in the nearby town of Lawrence and take them home. Papa had dropped off all the kids at their homes and was getting on the highway for his forty-five minute drive home when he had a heart attack and pulled over.

Papa was rushed to the hospital E.R. in Lawrence and when we got there they were trying to revive him for the second time already. They told us that he was not going to make it. I remember it so vividly. I was standing in the hallway, and I started talking to God, pacing, and whispering and to him. I was praying for God's grace and knowledge to be within the doctors and nurses, asking the Lord God to intervene through his great mercy, as the curtain was drawn around Papa while they did everything they could do to help him.

After a long forty minutes of waiting and then being feet away hearing all the people behind the curtain working on Papa, I was in fear of the unknown. I was asking for his grace, his glory, and for Christ to forgive Papa and remove all the sins within him to make him holy once again. The doctors and nurses in this emergency room in Lawrence were so kind and told us some amazing things about how strong Papa was. It made me smile, for God was with him in that moment with all those helping him as well. They managed to get his heart going and he was somewhat stabilized. Unfortunately the whole episode had left Papa with major damage to most of his bodily functions, and they thought he was not going to recover.

We visited the ICU every day for quite some time, and one of us stayed there all day and night. Papa was on a breathing machine, and despite the constant efforts of the medical staff, each day passed with no improvement. After some time, praying every day and night, one particular night I was home and walking the dog, and I had one of those feelings come over me. It was overwhelming, like I was in sort of a fog, and I broke down and cried, feeling some sort of an amazing inner connection to God in my mind and soul. Whatever was happening outside of me, whatever the dog was doing, I was only vaguely aware. I prayed, "Lord, do your best in helping Papa." I know that in some ways, that is a funny prayer. Of course, the Lord is going to do his best. How could he not? And his best is always *the* best. He's perfect! But I think I just meant, "Lord, I want you to do the best for my father-in-law, whatever the best is." I wanted God to heal him, asking the Lord over and over, but I did not know what the Lord wanted. What I was trying to say was, "Let your will be done."

That night I felt the Lord's presence as I rested praying to the Lord in my bed for hours. I had a powerful sense of enlightenment as though I was still connected to him from previously walking the dog, as though I was still praying well into the night. At some point I fell asleep and when I awoke in the morning, there was a powerful feeling within me. I had an overwhelming sense of rejoicing and something like a premonition, a strong feeling like intuition. I told my wife, "Something is very different today, Shay." I remember just shaking my head and trying to control myself so that I would not burst into tears. All morning I just kept saying, "something is very different."

I was still in awe of what had happened the night before and I did not want to overstate my knowledge, but I did want to gracefully explain to Shannon what I knew. Calmly and lovingly I proceeded to do so, though I was still uncertain. I felt like Thomas who wanted the confirmation of seeing and touching the holes in Christ's hands, feet, and side.

My confirmation came when we were in the waiting room later that day visiting Papa, and the doctors came in to tell us that they had been able to take Papa off the ventilator the night before. This seemed to the doctors like a miraculous recovery. Based on their experience, this was a near impossibility. This had profound meaning for Shannon and me, given our discussions of what the Lord had done the night before. I felt deeply that the Lord was giving him the chance to recover enough to say goodbye to his loved ones and to allow all of us to say goodbye to him, love him, and to be with him a little longer.

In his great mercy, God gave us a few more months with Papa, and I continued to experience considerable power, acknowledgement, from the presence of God when I prayed for Papa every week. When it comes to prayer, it matters less that your prayers are answered and more that you are able to get intimate with our Lord God Almighty and learn to relate to him and hear his voice. God will always do his will, but he graciously allows us to connect with him intimately through his will. The connection, the communication, the feeling, the hearing of Christ in prayer are the most important things, and from there everything is amazing with his grace in you. More on that later.

More Amazing Grace

I want to share another one. Several years ago my own father was diagnosed with pancreatic cancer. My parents lived down in Florida by then and had for some time. Once again I got that same sensation, that nudge that God was up to something and was calling me to intercession. My dad was about to have what is called a Whipple surgery to remove the pancreatic tumors. This is a very difficult and dangerous procedure with a comparatively low success rate. The doctors have to carve out most of the patient's insides to get to, and then take out the tumors. This means a partial removal of the stomach and the intestines. Life expectancy after this surgery in the last 20 to 40 years has gone from 5% to 50-70%.

I was in a field behind my house praying for my dad, and I had a strong feeling that he would survive the surgery. I flew down to Florida to be with my mom and sit with her and my dad in the ICU, as he lay there looking nearly dead with seven organ drainage tubes coming out of him. In the natural, we both thought he didn't look like he would make it. But one night, a strong sense came over me that he would indeed recover. I just knew it.

When these things happen, people who know me think it is because of my diabetic NDE experiences with God, but I do not think so. I don't think it is about that at all. God is amazing, and prayer is his amazing gift to us, because our connection to the Father is important to him. It happens in various ways, and it doesn't happen all the time, but anyone who will commit to taking time out each day and settling in to have a deep conversation with him through prayer will experience amazing things.

In his book, *I Heard God Laugh,* Matthew Kelly explains that to pray you just have to keep on trying. To me the act of praying is like trying to hit a baseball. You might not actually get a hit every time, but you just need to keep on getting up to the plate. You need to keep trying. You might need a little help from a hitting coach. My strong feeling is that many Christians were never taught how to pray and connect to God; they were never taught how to "swing the bat and hit the ball."

I feel this as a tragic misfortune for most Christians. When you know there is the ability to feel the presence of God and his love as you pray, to hear him speak to you, repeating a word to your mind, you can't get enough of it. When you have experienced the strong sense of the presence of the Holy Spirit within you during prayer, and when you have seen the miraculous sign of his answers to your prayers, you can't imagine following God any other way. As one who experiences God, I desperately want my friends and family to know him like I do, to experience the blessing of his presence and his help. I want them to know how to pray, when to listen, where to find God in prayer. So few Christians have been taught to pray in such a way. They have never had even a clue of the amazing connection with God that is possible to any of us by faith and a little intention.

My dad survived his operation. I was so happy, thanking God and overwhelmed that he left the hospital. Seeing how dire the situation was on the third day after his surgery, I could have lost hope. He certainly looked like he was not going to make it. That was the opinion of the doctors for sure. But he left the ICU, and then he left the hospital entirely. I experienced a tremendous feeling of elation as I raised my head and hands to God that day and praised his glorious name for his goodness and favor.

My dad did not fully recover. His cancer had already metastasized throughout his body, though they discovered this a month or two after his surgery. They told us he would live only two or three weeks after that, and my mom was calling for my brothers and me to come to Florida to say our last goodbyes. It brings tears to my eyes to write this today. All who have suffered the loss of close family members or friends will understand the emotional pain and major grief involved.

I remember later, standing in my front yard speaking on the phone with the doctor. I wanted to understand the full diagnosis before flying down. The confirmation from the doctor about the gravity of the situation wrenched my guts out on the lawn.

I entered that familiar state as we spoke. The fog came over me, the strong sense of a presence. When the Israelites were in the presence of God, there was a fog. In 2 Chronicles 5:13-14 it says,

> 13 and it was the duty of the trumpeters and singers to make themselves heard in unison in praise and thanksgiving to the Lord), and when the song was raised, with trumpets and cymbals and other musical instruments, in praise to the Lord,

"For he is good, for his steadfast love endures forever," the house, the house of the Lord, was filled with a cloud, 14 so that the priests could not stand to minister because of the cloud, for the glory of the Lord filled the house of God.

And then when Isaiah saw the Lord in his throne room it says, "And the foundations of the thresholds shook at the voice of him who called, and the house was filled with smoke" (Isa 6:4).

This fog was physical, but mine was spiritual, invisible. Still, the glory and presence of the Lord is what it felt like. He was with me and on me as I spoke with the doctor. The doc was Jewish, and I felt a feeling of gratitude as I thanked him for his ability to save my dad through the surgery so that he could have another four to eight weeks with him. I was so overwhelmed as I encouraged him and told him that God had blessed him to be able to help so many people through God's grace and for God's glory. Our shared faith in the God of Abraham brought a profound sense of God's presence in the conversation. I believe he also felt that this was no ordinary call, but that we were encountering God in it. We both understood that we would never forget that moment.

Full of the Holy Spirit as I got off the call, I was completely overcome with the need to turn to deep prayer. This would be one of those highly emotional prayers that happen to me sometimes. I begged the Lord for his mercy, his grace, and his glory in helping my dad. I was blown away by what I saw in my mind's eye as I prayed, weeping in my front yard talking to God! I have experienced God so many times and in so many extraordinary ways, but *this* was greater than anything I had ever experienced. Reflecting on it now, I see that it was absolutely some kind of sign with great symbolic meaning.

As I said, I was crying; the tears were streaming down my face in a torrential downpour. I wiped my face to dry my tears, and then I looked at my tears on my hand. On my finger, right before my eyes, one of my tears turned instantly black! The teardrop was cylindrical in a way, and it looked like a pencil lead, but deeper, richer, black. It frightened me as I looked in disbelief. Imagine the shock and fear you feel if you look and see a wasp on your finger. I immediately and violently flung it to the ground.

I then collected myself and I felt a sense within me that God was saying he is going to be with me. It was an acknowledgment that God was going to take my dad, and my last goodbyes were coming soon. I'm still not sure what to make of the teardrop, but I suppose black could signify death. It was a beautiful deep blackness, and I believed God was saying that my father would be allowed a beautiful death. But it was a tear, because even a beautiful death brings profound grief to those of us left behind.

The next day I flew to Florida. A plane is a good enough place to experience God, and another overwhelming feeling struck me, and I found myself again in the presence of God. The understanding was deepening inside me that my dad was going to die and be with God. But at the same time a sense of joy began to come over me, and I made my request to God as I moved through various stages of prayer on the plane ride sitting against the window gazing out at God's magnificent creation. I said, "God, do me a favor. Let me have a blessed moment with my dad during my short visit." I was not then fully aware of what grave condition he was in already. I said, "Please allow me to have a moment with my dad that we can share with each other and let your grace flow upon each of us in that moment. Through the covenant I ask this in Jesus' name, Father."

I arrived at the condo and entered my father's room. My brothers were there in another room. They had a hospice chaplain there and he came in and took me and my mother's hands as we performed healing prayer over my dad, and I was moved to make the sign of the cross over his forehead as we prayed over him.

Suddenly, my father was quite alert, his wits about him, and we talked for quite a while. He was more than coherent. That was such a blessing, but what was more amazing was what happened next. You may not think it is a big thing, but to me it was huge. At some point I asked my dad what he wanted. My mother had told me that over the last week, he could not hold anything down. He tried to eat or drink, but whatever he had he just threw back up. I asked him again when he didn't answer right away. Something inside told me I was supposed to ask. My dad at first said he did not understand, so I asked him again, "what do you want," and GRACE hit me. I'm not sure why, but a pleasant thought came to me, and I said to my dad, "would you like a cup of coffee?" He said, "Yes," that he would like to have a cup of coffee with me, and on the inside, it was like I was giggling!

My mom was giving me "the look." Does your mom do the look? Then you know what I'm talking about. She was showing me on her face that this was not a good idea. But I had a good feeling about it! I thought it was going to turn out to be a very good idea. I know how much my dad loved coffee, so I was excited and somehow not surprised that he said yes. The huge smile on my dad's face was worth facing down "the look." My mom could see not to disrupt the moment we were having, so she sat there in complete shock as she saw he was not getting sick. We were laughing and enjoying our coffees together, and I knew we were having the moment that I had asked for. God was granting my request!

As we continued to sip our coffee together, I could not stop thanking and praising God for his kindness toward us. The next morning, I went to the well again. Back at my mom and dad's condo I asked my dad if he'd like another cup of coffee. Again I was rewarded with a huge smile. This beaming was even bigger than the day before. He again said that he would love another cup of coffee. I saw my mom's jaw drop for the second time as she watched my dad and me enjoy an amazing time together as we drank our morning coffee.

Then my mom left the room for something, and I was able to talk to my dad in private. I didn't have much time, so I said to him, "I want you to know that you need not worry. Soon, in a few days, you're going to be with God, and it's going to be remarkable." Later that morning when I left to catch my flight back to Boston, it was strange. I wasn't going to be able to see him anymore. It was extremely painful to leave the house, hugging my brothers in the living room and then stopping at my dad's open bedroom door to say, "I will certainly see you very soon." I wasn't sure he knew what the statement meant, but I sure did. And I know he does now. I blew him a kiss and gave him a thumbs up as I walked away and left the condo. I came home and several days later I got the call from my mom at work. My dad had passed away peacefully. Shannon and I went back to Florida, and for the next several weeks I helped my mom with arrangements and paperwork while we all grieved together.

> I of course have tears running down my face now as I write this and remember. I want you to understand the grace and glory of God and how unbelievably amazing his love is for you. It is ASTONISHING!

One thing I learned over the years when it comes to death and grieving is that it happens quickly sometimes and is extremely painful. Handling grief on your own is the most painful. At times, the pain for me in the loss of a loved one was so powerful that I was driven to seek Christ in prayer. After all, Christ is "acquainted with grief" (Isa ?). Most people who know the Bible can tell you what the shortest verse in all of Scripture is, "Jesus wept." When his good friend Lazarus, the brother of Mary and Martha died, Jesus was going to raise him from the dead. In fact it says that he delayed coming to his aid when called for, because he knew he was supposed to perform this miracle. He knew how it ended!

And yet, arriving on the scene, seeing Lazarus' distraught family, the perfect son of God was overcome, and he wept (Jn ?). I pray to Christ when I am overwhelmed by pain and grief, and I ask for his grace. Though, like Jesus, we know how death ends. Christ defeated death on the cross so that one day, the ultimate end of death will come. Revelation 20:13-14 it says,

> 13 And the sea gave up the dead which were in it; and death and hell delivered up the dead which were in them: and they were judged every man according to their works. 14 And **death and hell were cast into the lake of fire.** This is the second death. (KJV emphasis added)

Death is personified at the last judgment and death will be no more. This is glorious news, and it means our grief for loved ones who have died in Christ is brief. In my NDE, being with God was so unbelievable. Many of those who have NDEs explain that they no longer fear death, because being with God is so amazing. We now know what it's like to be in his presence where there are *no worries, no pain,* and a pure, simple love with you completely. Understandably someone would not fear death after that. You know where you are going, and you can't wait to get there. This is the exact opposite of fear!

Sorrow and Pain

When my pain is overwhelming, I pray to Christ and ask for his grace, peace, and for comfort from his acknowledgment, and it has helped me tremendously. Christ knows what it is like to grieve and feel pain. Philip Yancy points out in his book, *The Jesus I Never Knew*, that we have a Savior who understands what it is like to be human in a broken, painful, fallen world. He points out that if we only had the Old Testament, we'd be like Job in his own intense grief, asking, 4 "Have you eyes of flesh? Do you see as man sees? 5 Are your days as the days of man, or your years as a man's years" (Job 10:4-5)?

But Jesus did have "eyes of flesh." He did experience what it is like to suffer as a man. He felt pain and grief more than anyone. I pray to Christ while I'm in such pain and overwhelmed. I ask him for grace, peace, and comfort from his acknowledgment of my suffering. I can truly attest to the fact that it has helped me tremendously to have Christ alongside me, knowing what he has been through and that he knows what it is like to grieve and suffer. In this way, I am never fully alone, never alone when I am in these times of grieving such as when I lose a close family member or friend.

If you are in a time of anguish, pain, and grief like this, pray to Christ Almighty. He knows, and he is with you. Not only that, but he loves and adores you. No one wants grief, but I believe there is grace in it. You can have the attachment, acknowledgment, and embodiment of Christ when you pray in your grief. My great hope for you who are reading this is that you will know you are never alone in your pain and grief. Christ is there with you, thrust me!

Amazing Healing

I had been involved with a team of coworkers for about two years at my job. We were dealing with a major commercial production of insulin pens for world distribution. I was the project engineer for the development. One day in the middle of this project, Jenn a good friend and coworker was not looking so well. I knew this woman well, having become her good friend over the first part of the project. She was extremely pale and looked like she had been up crying all night.

I felt overwhelmed and came over to her to ask what was wrong. She told me that her two-year-old daughter Lillie had an illness that caused sores throughout her entire mouth and throat, every area completely covered. They had been going back and forth to the emergency room for several days, but because Lillie was so young, they had not been able to give her the medicine that would have helped her. The poor thing could not swallow any fluid or food, because if she did, the pain was unbearable.

Jenn, my dear friend, was at her wit's end, drained, and weeping in front of me. She was exhausted from having tried everything she possibly could for her daughter. It was painful to hear about the pain the little girl was in, and almost as painful to see how badly it affected her poor mother, who was powerless to help her baby girl. After Jenn told me this, I held her hand and told her I was going to pray for her and her young daughter that very night. I said, of course, that I hoped she would get better soon and that I would be sure to check on her each day.

As happens to me, I was on my way home from work and I started praying for this little girl. I was deep into prayer, asking Christ to enter this child as she slept, to bring his glory and grace into her and slowly eradicate the sores within her mouth and down her throat. I asked him to give her peace and rest through the night and to help sleep and rest within the Lord. I remember that I was crying so hard that I had to pull over to the side of the road just outside my house. The intensity of this prayer had put me in such a state, and I felt the connection with God that told me the Lord was with me in a whole new way. All night in my bed I was awake praying for this girl.

The next morning, I drove into work saying my morning prayers, and in the asking phase I spoke of this little girl Lillie, asking again for her healing and Christ's love. I was at a different location that morning at work on a major program and away from Jenn's office. Late in the morning, I was back in the other facility close to Jenn's office, and I started getting frantic texts and emails, lots of them, saying, "Come to my office now!"

Alarmed, I stopped what I was doing and went up to my friend's office. As I approached her desk, I noticed she looked as terrible as the day before, like a mom distressed. Upon seeing me she sprang up from her desk, nearly shouting, "What did you do!" She was weeping as she cried again, "what did you do!" She had an expression that I read as intense sorrow, mixed with amazement as though she were in awe and disbelief. I truly could not tell if I was seeing joy or harsh sadness.

I answered, "What do you mean?"

She asked again, "What did you do?"

I paused for a moment and then answered, "I prayed intently to our Lord Jesus Christ through most of the night and early this morning for you, Jenn, and for your daughter Lillie, like I told I would yesterday. I asked the Lord to give her peace so she could sleep and to heal her from within."

Jenn was crying, telling me her daughter, Lillie, was healing. She said her sores had started to go away in the morning and were almost completely gone. Her mother was taking care of Lilly and had told her this morning that Lilly was eating popsicles, pain free and happily. By lunchtime all the sores were completely gone, and I smiled, gleaming in profound rejoice, because I knew from the connection with our Lord on the side of the road the night before.

Intercessors in the Bible

Prayer has been a key feature of human existence for believers since the beginning. We know Adam walked and talked with God. We know others did as well, but intercession really takes off with Abraham. Abraham was a man in the Middle East who God called to himself in order to establish a people. God's redemptive plan for the world was to save it by the vicarious death of Christ for the sins of the world. By "vicarious" I mean "acting or done for another" (*Oxford Dictionary*). Much about our faith concerns this concept of vicariousness. Adam sinned, so we are all sinners. 1 Corinthians 15:22 says, "For as in Adam all die, so also in Christ shall all be made alive." Adam was the delegated head of the world. By giving the world over to Satan, sin, and darkness, he brought the whole creation present and future down with him, us included. We are born "in Adam," therefore, we all are afflicted with his condition, which of course we prove immediately by committing our own sins.

But the glorious good news is that the same principle applies to our salvation, which was always God's plan since before the foundation of the world, "in Christ, shall all be made alive!"

I made that beautiful tangent (beautiful, because what's more beautiful than the gospel that saves?) because we were discussing Abraham.

Abraham was a type of Christ. Typology is one cool thing about the Bible. You can see Christ everywhere in the Old Testament when you start thinking about "types." Not only was Abraham a type of Christ, but so was Moses, Noah, and anyone else who showed up as a kind (or "type") of Savior from God. But it was not only people that were types for Christ, but also objects, like the ark of Noah: getting "in" the ark saved the "chosen people," Noah's family, who themselves were vicarious representatives of the whole human race, just like getting "in Christ" saves the "chosen people" of the Church.

Let's stay on this tangent just for fun. The Passover Lamb was a type of Christ. This was clear when Jesus preempted it by the broken bread and poured wine at the Last Supper when he instituted communion. He became the new Passover lamb. Tim Keller, who I quoted in an earlier chapter, wrote of this, and came up with a powerful list that illustrates the idea.

> "Jesus is the true and better Adam, who passed the test in the garden and whose obedience is imputed to us (1 Corinthians 15).
>
> Jesus is the true and better Abel, who, though innocently slain, has blood that cries out for our acquittal, not our condemnation (Hebrews 12:24).
>
> Jesus is the true and better Abraham, who answered the call of God to leave the comfortable and familiar and go out into the void "not knowing whither he went" to create a new people of God.
>
> Jesus is the true and better Isaac, who was not just offered up by his father on the mount but was truly sacrificed for us all.

God said to Abraham, "Now I know you love me, because you did not withhold your son, your only son whom you love, from me." Now we can say to God, "Now we know that you love us, because you did not withhold your son, your only son whom you love, from us."

Jesus is the true and better Jacob, who wrestled with God and took the blow of justice we deserved so that we, like Jacob, receive only the wounds of grace to wake us up and discipline us.

Jesus is the true and better Joseph, who at the right hand of the King forgives those who betrayed and sold him and uses his new power to save them.

Jesus is the true and better Moses, who stands in the gap between the people and the Lord and who mediates a new covenant (Hebrews 3).

Jesus is the true and better rock of Moses, who, struck with the rod of God's justice, now gives us water in the desert.

Jesus is the true and better Job - the truly innocent sufferer - who then intercedes for and saves his stupid friends (Job 42).

Jesus is the true and better David, whose victory becomes his people's victory, though they never lifted a stone to accomplish it themselves.

Jesus is the true and better Esther, who didn't just risk losing an earthly palace but lost the ultimate heavenly one, who didn't just risk his life but gave his life—to save his people.

Jesus is the true and better Jonah, who was cast out into the storm so we could be brought in." (Timothy J. Keller, Preaching: Communicating Faith in an Age of Skepticism)

Abraham is a type, and his intercession for Lot and Sodom is a type — because Jesus is the great intercessor at the right hand of God, and if we pray for others, we too become types, or representatives, or even vicarious persons as we pray on their behalf. Is that not amazing!
It's enough that God created us, loves us, sent Jesus to die for us, wants us to abide with him forever, *but he also LETS us help him with his purposes.* We get to perform a powerful role when we get to speak in Jesus' name in our prayers. It is so cool when you think about it.

My hope is that you will catch the prayer bug, because I truly believe that the more of God's people who will take up the mantle and exercise their privilege as the royal priesthood (1 Pt 2:9) that God calls us and pray to him, the more the world will be filled with God's light and glory.

I believe that God is in control. I believe that he gets his way, *and yet,* Jesus taught us that God's will is ordinarily done only in a certain way on earth. When he taught us to pray, "Our Father in heaven…Thy *will be done on earth* as it is *in heaven…*" he was teaching us that it would be an amazing thing for God's will to happen on earth in some way different than how it usually is. God wants things to happen on earth and he has *ordained* that they will not happen until we pray for them.

Here are some biblical examples of what I mean. In the first example, God had rescued the Israelites from slavery in Egypt in such a mighty and miraculous way, that it's hard to imagine why they could have constantly doubted him and disobeyed him in the wilderness. God made a covenant with them, promising to bless them beyond imagination if only they would follow his righteous ways. His ways were good. He wanted them to obey him, because he wanted them to live abundant lives in the Promised Land. Here are some of his promises in Deut 28:

> 1 "And if you faithfully obey the voice of the Lord your God, being careful to do all his commandments that I command you today, the Lord your God will set you high above all the nations of the earth. 2 And all these blessings shall come upon you and overtake you, if you obey the voice of the Lord your God. 3 Blessed shall you be in the city, and blessed shall you be in the field. 4 Blessed shall be the fruit of your womb and the fruit of your ground and the fruit of your cattle, the increase of your herds and the young of your flock. 5 Blessed shall be your basket and your kneading bowl. 6 Blessed shall you be when you come in, and blessed shall you be when you go out.
>
> 7 "The Lord will cause your enemies who rise against you to be defeated before you. They shall come out against you one way and flee before you seven ways. 8 The Lord will command the blessing on you in your barns and in all that you undertake. And he will bless you in the land that the Lord your God is giving you. 9 The Lord will establish you as a people holy to himself, as he has sworn to you, if you keep the commandments of the Lord your God and walk in his ways. 10 And all the peoples of the earth shall see that you are called by the name of the Lord, and they shall be afraid of you. 11 And the Lord will make you abound in prosperity, in the fruit of your womb and in the fruit of your livestock and in the fruit of your ground, within the land that the Lord swore to your fathers to give you. 12 The Lord will open to you his good treasury, the heavens, to give the rain to your land in its season and to bless all the work of your hands. And you shall lend to many nations, but you shall

> not borrow. 13 And the Lord will make you the head and not the tail, and you shall only go up and not down, if you obey the commandments of the Lord your God, which I command you today, being careful to do them, 14 and if you do not turn aside from any of the words that I command you today, to the right hand or to the left, to go after other gods to serve them. (Deut 28:1-14)

It is awesome to see all the good plans God had for his people. He had already rescued them with the promise of a land of their own, and now all these wonderful blessings are promised on top of that.

However, there was another side of the coin. God is perfectly just, and he has created a world governed by his laws. His moral law is in the Bible, but this also includes the laws of nature, the laws of reality and cause and effect. God designed the world and man a certain way, and there is no way around pain if you decide not to accept that. This is manifested concretely in his law for the Israelites and the consequences given for disobeying that law.

Curses for Disobedience

> 15 "But if you will not obey the voice of the Lord your God or be careful to do all his commandments and his statutes that I command you today, then all these curses shall come upon you and overtake you. 16 Cursed shall you be in the city, and cursed shall you be in the field. 17 Cursed shall be your basket and your kneading bowl. 18 Cursed shall be the fruit of your womb and the fruit of your ground, the increase of your herds and the young of your flock. 19 Cursed shall you be when you come in, and cursed shall you be when you go out."

20 "The Lord will send on you curses, confusion, and frustration in all that you undertake to do, until you are destroyed and perish quickly on account of the evil of your deeds, because you have forsaken me. 21 The Lord will make the pestilence stick to you until he has consumed you off the land that you are entering to take possession of it. 22 The Lord will strike you with wasting disease and with fever, inflammation and fiery heat, and with drought[a] and with blight and with mildew. They shall pursue you until you perish. 23 And the heavens over your head shall be bronze, and the earth under you shall be iron. 24 The Lord will make the rain of your land powder. From heaven dust shall come down on you until you are destroyed."

25 "The Lord will cause you to be defeated before your enemies. You shall go out one way against them and flee seven ways before them. And you shall be a horror to all the kingdoms of the earth. 26 And your dead body shall be food for all birds of the air and for the beasts of the earth, and there shall be no one to frighten them away. 27 The Lord will strike you with the boils of Egypt, and with tumors and scabs and itch, of which you cannot be healed. 28 The Lord will strike you with madness and blindness and confusion of mind, 29 and you shall grope at noonday, as the blind grope in darkness, and you shall not prosper in your ways. And you shall be only oppressed and robbed continually, and there shall be no one to help you. 30 You shall betroth a wife, but another man shall ravish her. You shall build a house, but you shall not dwell in it. You shall plant a vineyard, but you shall not enjoy its fruit. 31 Your ox shall be slaughtered before your eyes, but you shall not eat any of it. Your donkey shall be seized before your face, but shall not be restored to you. Your sheep shall be given to your enemies, but there shall be no one to help you. 32 Your sons and your daughters shall be given to

another people, while your eyes look on and fail with longing for them all day long, but you shall be helpless. 33 A nation that you have not known shall eat up the fruit of your ground and of all your labors, and you shall be only oppressed and crushed continually, 34 so that you are driven mad by the sights that your eyes see. 35 The Lord will strike you on the knees and on the legs with grievous boils of which you cannot be healed, from the sole of your foot to the crown of your head."

36 "The Lord will bring you and your king whom you set over you to a nation that neither you nor your fathers have known. And there you shall serve other gods of wood and stone. 37 And you shall become a horror, a proverb, and a byword among all the peoples where the Lord will lead you away. 38 You shall carry much seed into the field and shall gather in little, for the locust shall consume it. 39 You shall plant vineyards and dress them, but you shall neither drink of the wine nor gather the grapes, for the worm shall eat them. 40 You shall have olive trees throughout all your territory, but you shall not anoint yourself with the oil, for your olives shall drop off. 41 You shall father sons and daughters, but they shall not be yours, for they shall go into captivity. 42 The cricket[c] shall possess all your trees and the fruit of your ground. 43 The sojourner who is among you shall rise higher and higher above you, and you shall come down lower and lower. 44 He shall lend to you, and you shall not lend to him. He shall be the head, and you shall be the tail."

45 "All these curses shall come upon you and pursue you and overtake you till you are destroyed, because you did not obey the voice of the Lord your God, to keep his commandments and his statutes that he commanded you. 46 They shall be a sign and a wonder against you and your offspring forever. 47 Because you

did not serve the Lord your God with joyfulness and gladness of heart, because of the abundance of all things, 48 therefore you shall serve your enemies whom the Lord will send against you, in hunger and thirst, in nakedness, and lacking everything. And he will put a yoke of iron on your neck until he has destroyed you. 49 The Lord will bring a nation against you from far away, from the end of the earth, swooping down like the eagle, a nation whose language you do not understand, 50 a hard-faced nation who shall not respect the old or show mercy to the young. 51 It shall eat the offspring of your cattle and the fruit of your ground, until you are destroyed; it also shall not leave you grain, wine, or oil, the increase of your herds or the young of your flock, until they have caused you to perish."

52 "They shall besiege you in all your towns, until your high and fortified walls, in which you trusted, come down throughout all your land. And they shall besiege you in all your towns throughout all your land, which the Lord your God has given you. 53 And you shall eat the fruit of your womb, the flesh of your sons and daughters, whom the Lord your God has given you, in the siege and in the distress with which your enemies shall distress you. 54 The man who is the most tender and refined among you will begrudge food to his brother, to the wife he embraces,[d] and to the last of the children whom he has left, 55 so that he will not give to any of them any of the flesh of his children whom he is eating, because he has nothing else left, in the siege and in the distress with which your enemy shall distress you in all your towns. 56 The most tender and refined woman among you, who would not venture to set the sole of her foot on the ground because she is so delicate and tender, will begrudge to the husband she embraces,[e] to her son and to her daughter, 57 her afterbirth that comes out from between her feet

and her children whom she bears, because lacking everything she will eat them secretly, in the siege and in the distress with which your enemy shall distress you in your towns."

58 "If you are not careful to do all the words of this law that are written in this book, that you may fear this glorious and awesome name, the Lord your God, 59 then the Lord will bring on you and your offspring extraordinary afflictions, afflictions severe and lasting, and sicknesses grievous and lasting. 60 And he will bring upon you again all the diseases of Egypt, of which you were afraid, and they shall cling to you. 61 Every sickness also and every affliction that is not recorded in the book of this law, the Lord will bring upon you, until you are destroyed. 62 Whereas you were as numerous as the stars of heaven, you shall be left few in number, because you did not obey the voice of the Lord your God. 63 And as the Lord took delight in doing you good and multiplying you, so the Lord will take delight in bringing ruin upon you and destroying you. And you shall be plucked off the land that you are entering to take possession of it."

64 "And the Lord will scatter you among all peoples, from one end of the earth to the other, and there you shall serve other gods of wood and stone, which neither you nor your fathers have known. 65 And among these nations you shall find no respite, and there shall be no resting place for the sole of your foot, but the Lord will give you there a trembling heart and failing eyes and a languishing soul. 66 Your life shall hang in doubt before you. Night and day you shall be in dread and have no assurance of your life. 67 In the morning you shall say, 'If only it were evening!' and at evening you shall say, 'If only it were morning!' because of the dread that your heart shall feel, and the sights

that your eyes shall see. 68 And the Lord will bring you back in ships to Egypt, a journey that I promised that you should never make again; and there you shall offer yourselves for sale to your enemies as male and female slaves, but there will be no buyer." (Deut 28:15-68)

If you read all that, *way to go!* But even if you didn't, you get the drift, I'm sure. God is showing that by no means is he unjust. He is showing that the world runs in large part by cause and effect. If you do this, then he will do that. Or if you do this, then this will happen to you. Whenever we suffer the consequences of our actions, we are seeing this principle at play. Even when we seem to suffer with apparent reason, for instance, we are born with type one diabetes like I was, it should still be considered the consequences of sin in the world. This is part of the deep mystery of the doctrine of original sin. "As in Adam all die…" Whenever bad things happen, one answer that works every time to answer the question "why" is that it is because of sin—the world is fallen.

But before I lose my point, my aim is to show that *even though* the Israelites opted for option B, disobeying God, and receiving the promised curses, God was still faithful to them based on his own love for fulfilling his ultimate purposes. But let's not forget that our topic right now is intercession. In one particular instance of breathtaking concretization, we see both God's desire to save them despite their disobedience *and* his tendency to use the intercessory prayers of one of his faithful servants.

Here's what happened. Moses had been summoned to Mount Sinai to receive the law from God. He'd been up there for forty days. God did not allow anyone to come near the mountain, because he was taking the opportunity to teach his people about his utter holiness, and humanity's need for him. It is our fallen nature that causes our greatest need for God. So his warning was because he knew how "unclean" they still were in their sin. He knew that if he let them approach the holy ground of the place where he was dwelling, they would die. He cleansed Moses but in order for Moses to come up, and Joshua to come only part way. The rest of the Israelites were warned to stay away.

As a side note, don't gloss over these kinds of passages because they are scary or because they make God seem terrifying and unapproachable. God *is* terrifying and unapproachable *except for one thing*. He has sent his Son to die for our sins and to *give us for free his righteousness*. Ro 3:20-21 tells us,

> 20 For by works of the law no human being will be justified in his sight, since through the law comes knowledge of sin.
>
> 21 But now the righteousness of God has been manifested apart from the law, although the Law and the Prophets bear witness to it—

That righteousness was Jesus Christ and he imputed it to us who have believed and repented of sin! This is made all the more profound and wonderful by the understanding of God's terrifying holiness as shown by his loving warning to the Israelites.

> 16 On the morning of the third day there were thunders and lightnings and a thick cloud on the mountain and a very loud trumpet blast, so that all the people in the camp trembled. 17 Then Moses brought the people out of the camp to meet God, and they took their stand at the foot of the mountain. 18 Now Mount Sinai was wrapped in smoke because the Lord had descended on it in fire. The smoke of it went up like the smoke of a kiln, and the whole mountain trembled greatly. 19 And as the sound of the trumpet grew louder and louder, Moses spoke,

and God answered him in thunder. 20 The Lord came down on Mount Sinai, to the top of the mountain. And the Lord called Moses to the top of the mountain, and Moses went up.

21 And the Lord said to Moses, "Go down and warn the people, lest they break through to the Lord to look and many of them perish. 22 Also let the priests who come near to the Lord consecrate themselves, lest the Lord break out against them." 23 And Moses said to the Lord, "The people cannot come up to Mount Sinai, for you yourself warned us, saying, 'Set limits around the mountain and consecrate it.'" 24 And the Lord said to him, "Go down, and come up bringing Aaron with you. But do not let the priests and the people break through to come up to the Lord, lest he break out against them." 25 So Moses went down to the people and told them. (Exodus 19:16-25 emphasis added)

But while Moses was up there receiving the law and the Ten Commandments, the people got nervous that he may not come back down. Human nature in our sin is so tragic. Look what happens.

1 When the people saw that Moses delayed to come down from the mountain, the people gathered themselves together to Aaron and said to him, "Up, make us gods who shall go before us. As for this Moses, the man who brought us up out of the land of Egypt, we do not know what has become of him." 2 So Aaron said to them, "Take off the rings of gold that are in the ears of your wives, your sons, and your daughters, and bring them to me." 3 So all the people took off the rings of gold that were in their ears and brought them to Aaron. 4 And he received the gold from their hand and fashioned it with a graving tool and made a golden[a] calf. And they said, "These are your gods, O

Israel, who brought you up out of the land of Egypt!" 5 When Aaron saw this, he built an altar before it. And Aaron made a proclamation and said, "Tomorrow shall be a feast to the Lord." 6 And they rose up early the next day and offered burnt offerings and brought peace offerings. And the people sat down to eat and drink and rose up to play.

7 And the Lord said to Moses, "Go down, for your people, whom you brought up out of the land of Egypt, have corrupted themselves. 8 They have turned aside quickly out of the way that I commanded them. They have made for themselves a golden calf and have worshiped it and sacrificed to it and said, 'These are your gods, O Israel, who brought you up out of the land of Egypt!'" 9 And the Lord said to Moses, "I have seen this people, and behold, it is a stiff-necked people. 10 Now therefore let me alone, that my wrath may burn hot against them, and I may consume them, in order that I may make a great nation of you." (Ex 32:1-10)

What is at stake here is the whole plan of the redemption of the world! How could things have gone so wrong so quickly? We're seeing here a glimpse of the human condition. Apart from the salvation of the Lord, this is what humans are like. One theologian put it this way: "The human heart is an idol factory" (Institutes I.11.8, John Calvin). Indeed it is. But before I lose my point, I want to move to what happens next. God had revealed to Moses his plan to wipe them out and start over. If you're paying attention you might be thinking, "But what about God's promises to Israel?" First, don't forget that he promised to discipline them if they rebelled. But you're right, he has been promising since Genesis 3 to save mankind (Gen 3), so now he's got a problem.

But he also has a solution: the intercession of a faithful man of prayer. Look what happens:

> 11 But Moses implored the Lord his God and said, "O Lord, why does your wrath burn hot against your people, whom you have brought out of the land of Egypt with great power and with a mighty hand? 12 Why should the Egyptians say, 'With evil intent did he bring them out, to kill them in the mountains and to consume them from the face of the earth'? Turn from your burning anger and relent from this disaster against your people. 13 Remember Abraham, Isaac, and Israel, your servants, to whom you swore by your own self, and said to them, 'I will multiply your offspring as the stars of heaven, and all this land that I have promised I will give to your offspring, and they shall inherit it forever.'" 14 **And the Lord relented from the disaster that he had spoken of bringing on his people.** (Emphasis added)

"And the Lord relented from the disaster that he had spoken of bringing on his people." God wanted to save his people, but he wanted Moses to pray first. This is an awesome example of the way God chooses to accomplish his will through the partnership of the prayers of his people.

Job

Another example of intercession in the Bible comes when God shows up at the end of the book of Job. Job has undergone a terrible trial, and when his friends arrive, they spend most of the book speaking wrongly of God. God corrects them after several chapters of displaying his glory over creation. But look what he says to them:

> 7 After the Lord had spoken these words to Job, the Lord said to Eliphaz the Temanite: "My anger burns against you and against your two friends, for you have not spoken of me what is right, as my servant Job has. 8 Now therefore take seven bulls and seven rams and go to my servant Job and offer up a burnt offering for yourselves. And my servant Job shall pray for you, for I will accept his prayer not to deal with you according to your folly. For you have not spoken of me what is right, as my servant Job has." 9 So Eliphaz the Temanite and Bildad the Shuhite and Zophar the Naamathite went and did what the Lord had told them, and the Lord accepted Job's prayer. (Job 42:7-9 emphasis added)

God wants to forgive them, but he makes it clear that he wants this to come about by the priestly activity of his intercessor, Job.

Daniel is another example. He is with the exiled Jews in Babylon, and he knows it is because the Israelites were being disciplined for their rebellion against God. Daniel goes so far as to repent on behalf of the nation.

> 3 Then I turned my face to the Lord God, seeking him by prayer and pleas for mercy with fasting and sackcloth and ashes. 4 I prayed to the Lord my God and made confession, saying, "O Lord, the great and awesome God, who keeps covenant and steadfast love with those who love him and keep his commandments, 5 we have sinned and done wrong and acted wickedly and rebelled, turning aside from your commandments and rules. 6 We have not listened to your servants the prophets, who spoke in your name to our kings, our princes, and our fathers, and to all the people of the land." (Dan 9:3-6 emphasis added)

Teach the Youth to Pray

I've seen God work in so many ways through prayer. Another time I was down in Hartford, CT. Some of the local churches where I live had gone down on a mission trip. If you have a week off sometime, I highly recommend doing something like that. I don't know who it helps more, the people you are serving, or you, as the person who God is using. It was an amazing experience.

We ran these faith formation activities each night throughout the week, and some remarkable things happened. At this particular mission there were around one-hundred fifty kids gathered from all over the country. On one of the nights, all of the chaperones were given a candle and instructed to sit in various places throughout the gymnasium. The places were marked with different faith statements on banners. One said, "peace," another said, "forgiveness," and there were others. I stationed myself at one of the spots in the back corner with my candle and my phone. It was dark in the room except for all these candles.

One-by-one the students were to walk in and get their own candle, choosing which of the chaperones they wanted to talk to. They could talk about anything they needed to concerning their sins, their issues, or anything else on their minds.

I was nervous. I was the only one on the bleachers, because I have back problems from a car accident long ago, and sitting on the floor like the other chaperones wasn't an option for me. I didn't know if any of the students were going to come over to me, and for twenty minutes, none of them did. But then, out of the darkness, came Evan, one of the students from my church. I actually felt elated to see him, and we spoke for ten minutes about his life and what he was planning to do the next year for college.

Then he asked for help. He said he had no connection to God, but he wanted one. I almost dropped to my knees in tears, and my soul was on fire! I could feel Christ calming me down and I felt his knowledge flow through me as things began to come to mind. I told Evan of prayer and how I connect with God every day when I pray, and I told him how he could do it, and that I would teach him more before he went off to college. I went over a typical prayer session a few times, and I asked him if it would be okay if I prayed over him. He said yes, so I prayed a short prayer asking God to open Evan's mind and through this knowledge to allow him to connect with the Lord in the days to come. I later sent him some books in the mail on prayer.

When Evan had walked away, another student from my parish came up to me, Ben. Ben asked me to pray over him for God to help him with his anxiety. The funny thing is that Ben didn't know that I also have anxiety and I often pray to Christ. I spoke a healing prayer, a request for Ben to feel a connection with God so that through Christ his anxiety could be healed. This prayer was flowing through me with loving statements and grace. God loves to work through us, and when we do, sometimes amazing things happen. I could tell that God was moving on Ben and he was feeling God's power too.

About a week after the trip, I got a text from Ben. He was screaming through the text in capital letters, because he was so excited. He finally called me and told me that he had been having an anxiety attack that almost paralyzed him. He remembered our prayer and he started to pray in the same way, *and Jesus showed up!* God helped him as he called out to Jesus. His anxiety and fear that was paralyzing him moments before, instantly went away, the worry and fear leaving his mind. Being his first major experience with Christ, he was overwhelmed. I reminded him of the prayer I had prayed over him and rejoiced that God had answered that prayer. I also reminded him that Christ is always with us every second of the day, and that we should attempt to pray every morning to the best of our ability. I texted him a copy of my prayer process, the same one I had given Evan, and I told him he will see things each week and see incremental changes in his life as a result if he would pray. I told him to open his spiritual eyes and feel Christ within him after prayer and after asking for God's will to be done, and that the result of Christ's love and abundance in his life would overflow to others!

My Prayer Process

I want to walk you through the process that I showed Ben and Evan. This is how I pray, and rarely do I not experience some measure of God's presence and peace. Whenever I pray I learn something about life. I completely submit myself to a life of service to God, say, "Lord, I surrender to you to do your will." I want to walk with him in the simplest way each day, with God's simplistic, pure love within me as I interact with others throughout each hour.

I hope you understand how this is prayer. In some ways, I am a man of only one thing: being in the presence of God. Everything else comes out of that. There is a priest in Connecticut named Father Rose, and I heard him make a statement when he was giving a homily during a mission trip I where I was a participant. The purpose of his statement was to help us realize some things about ourselves, our lives, and about God. Here are the five things he said in this statement:

1. Life is rough. Life is not easy, but difficult.
2. You are not important.
3. You are not in control.
4. The week (meaning that week we were on the mission trip) is not about you.
5. And yes, one day you are going to die.

Let me briefly address those five statements.

1. It is true that life is hard but: "My yoke is easy and my burden is light" (Mt 11:28). If your religion has no deep joy, no inherent contentment about it, then it is not the real thing. Life is hard for everyone, but it is infinitely harder without the presence of God in your life.

2. It is true that you are not that important, but, "Do you not know that your name is written in heaven" (Lk 10:20)? If we know our original blessing, we can handle our original sin. The soul needs meaning as much as the body needs food, but we live in an addictive society which constantly ups the ante of need and desire because the last ones have never satisfied. It is an understanding of true meaning that is the antidote to this vicious cycle.

3. It is true that your life is not about you: "I live not my own life, but the life of Christ who lives in me" (Gal 2:20). All the great people in history are characterized by "radical humility". The most courageous thing you will ever do is accept that you are just yourself. "Original sin is humanity's endless capacity for self-rejection" (Henri Nouwen). Note Jesus' story about a wedding banquet to which nobody wants to come! "Christ plays in ten thousand places,/Lovely in limbs, and lovely in eyes not his,/ To the Father through the features of men's faces" (Gerard Manley Hopkins).

4. It is true that you are not in control, but: "Can any of you for all your worrying, add a single moment to your span of life" (Lk 12:26)? Westerners are high-maintenance people. When you set yourselves up to think you deserve, expect, or need something

to happen, you are setting yourself up for constant unhappiness. Practice giving up control early in life. Surrender is a willingness to trust that you are really a beloved son, which allows God to be your Father. It really is that simple.

5. It is true that you are going to die, but: "Neither death nor life" can come between us and the love of God? (Romans 8:38-39). Yes, we are going to die, but death is not final - and it takes the form of love. We cannot make God love us any more, and we cannot make God love us less. So "it is heaven all the way to heaven" (Catherine of Siena). "Life is the destiny you are bound to refuse until you have consented to die" (Auden).

Reflecting on these statements has helped me when going into prayer to understand what I need in order to try to get Christ's help. It helps me to connect to Christ in my thoughts, feelings, and words. Every sentence, action, and deed is undertaken in the confirmation that he helps in so many different ways through the day. I acknowledge early in the morning before I head out that I am called to love my neighbor, thinking of all the interactions I will have with so many people throughout the day. Being with Christ early in the morning sets me up for an amazing ability to exhibit the overflowing love and grace of Christ in both my prayers and my encounters throughout the day.

This can be difficult in our lives with our long day of work and our family responsibilities. The statement above is hard, but it works. You might need to pause at times and reflect before your own will takes over and you react too quickly. Whisper Christ's name. This is my one moment advice, and early morning prayer makes this easier.

When you pause like that, it is your morning prayers that come back to you, and you are reminded of his presence. In that moment of an interaction with another person, this is vital if you want to reflect Christ to those around you. I try to remain in Christ no matter what, whispering his name as I walk, as I go into meetings, phone calls, or any other situation with others. I get enlightened prior to facing my next interaction, and it's amazing! Christ helps me from within with simplistic love from the first greeting of the encounter. You might find this to be intense after an hour in this state of glorification. You might not even remember all your interactions. You might feel consumed by the day. My advice is to use your drive home (if you have one) to reflect and pray in your car for a restoration alone in his presence. God's love will be present with you again for the ones you love the most, your family.

How I Pray

So in the early mornings, find a place that is quiet with no distractions to take you away from your internal thoughts. My room works for me, or my yard, or my side porch, which I call the East Wing. This wrap-around porch faces the eastern sky, and I can watch the sun rise up over the tree line and shine down on me as I sit in my chair and table with my coffee in the early morning. I pray with the sun on my face, sheltered on that side from the wind like I'm in a hidden sun room.

When I was on the mission trip, I went to pray every morning from 5-6 a.m. Afterward I walked off campus up to a baseball field and sat in the small set of bleachers looking again toward the east with the sunrise. During the workweek, my favorite place of all is in a town called Harvard. It's an overlook pullover spot that has a view of the valley down below with mountains in the distance. The 180 degree panoramic view is amazing. Most of the time I stop here on the way to work, pull over and turn the car off from 7-7:30 and pray with the rosary in my hands. If you are not Catholic, you might not know what that is, but it is a guided prayer process you can find online if you Google it.

Things always happen at this spot. I'm not sure why but they do. Prayer in my twenties was simple praying: "Thanks", "Sorry", "Please", steps of prayer while talking with God. I did not experience a major connection most of the time, but as I explained in earlier chapters, I had few occasions where I did.

Steps

I pray in steps. I prayed these steps early on, but I've learned from my reading that I was not at that time fully engaged in communication. I was not in deep prayer until the past several years when things became profound and experiential.

The length of my prayers now ranges from 5 to 30 minutes, depending on the time I'm praying. Sometimes intercessory praying takes hours and hours and is intense. I have a strong willingness for a connection with God and when I zero in on a focus point with him I can have many hours praying on another level. This is not forced or difficult. It is a purely glorified, almost miraculous connection that I struggle to describe.

I learned new daily prayer steps from a book by Matthew Kelly, *I Heard God Laugh.* His seven steps of prayer, his "prayer process" is helpful.

In baseball, the point is to get up to the plate and try to hit the ball every day. That is all you can do. You might hit the ball once or twice, but you need to get up to the plate as often as possible. Just as in baseball, you don't always connect, but every once in a while, you hit it so solid, and the ball jumps off the bat with a beautiful "crack" and just soars (think of golf as well). It's the same with prayer. You keep stepping up to the plate, and a full connection with Christ will happen. You may not tap in every time, but if you keep going to him you **will** find an amazing connection with God.

It must be said, those who experience God in their prayer life are those who have a prayer life. You can't shortcut the work of just going to him. Get seriously involved, make time every day. I suggest you start early in the morning, because after that first connection, you won't want to stop. You'll want to pray every day and seek to go into deeper and deeper connections. You will see things, hear things, and learn things in prayer as you build constant communication with God. You will see things throughout your day differently. People will look different, places will look different, and even animals will look different. You will have a new kind of joy and love flowing through you as Christ's love flows out of you to others. This is life at a DIFFERENT LEVEL! I PROMISE YOU! But you have to start.

Above, I mentioned Matthew Kelly's Prayer Process, and I'd like to share it with you. These sessions help me develop a deeper connection. I'm sharing all this with you, because I know you could look at my experiences with God in my NDE, and think that is why I can pray like I do. But I do not believe that these experiences are because of my NDEs. While my NDEs have given me some reference points for what the love of God feels like, I believe I could access God's Spirit, presence, and power just as well through this prayer process. Let this book serve as your reference point.

Process

I start by getting into one of my places already mentioned, and I find silence and peace. Then I may read a short devotional. As of this writing,

I am using ***Jesus Calling****: **Enjoying Peace in His Presence***, by Sarah Young. It is an amazing little book of short daily reflections to help you set up a connection with Christ for the day. Each day includes Jesus speaking to you as though he had written the book in first person, and it makes the perfect setup for prayer.

After that the in-depth conversation with God begins with the official "step one." I will do this process at least once a day, almost always in the morning, and sometimes again later in the day, depending on how long my workday is. If I have time, I'll stop on the way home and pray again so I can be ready to be with my loved ones in a greater Christ consciousness.

Step One: Gratitude

Thank God for:

- The first breath of your day
- For my life
- The people in your life
- The special people who dedicate themselves to God with Christ's love
- For your family
- For all that you have
- For his grace
- For his peace
- For his knowledge and revelation
- For his Word
- For his power
- For his glory

I say these words, "Thank you Lord of all creation. You are amazing and I thank you for everything in my life."

Let this come from the heart. Often by this point I will already have broken down crying. Gratitude is powerful and it should move you as you get more and more into it. God is so gracious and generous to us. Learn more and more to dig down deep and be truly grateful for what you've been given. If you are still alive, it's a gift. Even if you are going through hard times, learn to see those as a gift from God to bring you back to him for eternity, and ultimately, for your bliss. This step should become full and intense thanksgiving.

Step Two: Awareness

In step two, Kelly says, revisit the last 24 hours and ask God to show you when you were and when you were not in Christ or like Christ. Talk to God about these situations. Thank him for his grace for when you were in Christ and living lovingly, honestly, courageously, and faithfully. Talk to God about what you learned in the moments when you were not this way. This can be a powerful point of communication, because God loves honesty, he is the Truth, and he loves for us to get to the truth about ourselves.

Go over your interactions with people the day before. How did you treat them? Tell God what you did and why you did it. The Lord will fill you with his love and give you guidance on how you could have been in those moments. You should feel grace and love, and at certain times hear a thought or a word within you. A great man who I loved so much in my church, Deacon Pat, once told me, "We talk too much to God, but what we never do well is purely *listen*."

I find myself highly emotional and in tears sometimes in this section of prayer, thanking him for the knowledge, and most of the time I find myself taking immediate action after my prayer session is over to reconcile or seek forgiveness from someone by call, text, email, or a visit. I take Christlike action from his thought, his Word, his knowledge. It is unbelievable how I've seen God move in this section of the prayer. In these moments you are having a true connection with God, receiving the Lord's grace as he personally teaches you the way, the truth, and the life with him in prayer.

Step 3: Significant Moments

In this step or section of prayer you need to identify that day or the day before where God may have been at work. We know he is always working, but there are identifiable "God moments" if you pay attention to your day. It might be an event, a powerful feeling, or an interaction with a person. In this portion, I usually reflect on the Lord's amazing grace. I search for a moment that was profound and I could sense his awesome glory in the interaction. Perhaps it was a person loving you and helping you. Maybe it was a sign of his presence (I'll discuss this more later), or an instance of great beauty, such as a landscape, a mountain, a piece of God-inspired art or another creation. It will be something that amazes and inspires you. For me, it is usually an interaction with a person, and I thank the Lord for that moment.

Step 4: Peace

In this step of your prayer process, you are asking God for forgiveness for the wrong you have done against yourself, another person, or God himself. I should say, "and" God himself. You cannot sin against yourself or a person without sinning against God. He loves you that much. This is critical in starting your day. Review again the last 24-48 hours, reflect on them, and ask him for forgiveness.

I often become deeply sorrowful as I think of my actions and my will and how it drove me to do things that were not like Christ. As I go over the way I was, hurting others with my words and actions, I ask Christ to remove all these sins, these evil thoughts, and actions, to cleanse me of them and let his blood cover them. I ask him to lift them out of my mind and out of my soul and let them be on him on the cross. He said,

> 28 Come to me, all who labor and are heavy laden, and I will give you rest. 29 Take my yoke upon you, and learn from me, for I am gentle and lowly in heart, and you will find rest for your souls. 30 For my yoke is easy, and my burden is light. (Mt 11:28-30)

Christ can carry what we cannot. See yourself placing this burden on his infinitely strong shoulders. Feel the freedom of weightlessness as you give them over in repentance. An enlightening occurs, a pureness, and a feeling of peace overwhelms me. I may have felt a loving connection with him in the prior steps, but here I will feel it the most. I bless Christ then and thank him for his peace, grace, love, forgiveness, and his righteousness within me in my mind and soul. I ask him to continue to fill me and reign in me and through me for the rest of my day. This happens every single day.

Step 5: Freedom

In step 5 you must speak to God either in your mind or through speech. Ask him how he is inviting you to change your life in ways that will allow you to experience the freedom to be like Christ. In this section of the prayer process, I find myself remembering when I overflowed with love in the interactions of the recent days and when I noticed Christ in others so clearly. Nicky Gumbel from the Alpha Evangelism small group program where I have served at my church calls it "putting on the eyeglasses of Christ." You get to see and notice things that you would have never noticed or seen before.

This is a time of being in the glory of Christ as I speak to him. The reason this step is called "Freedom" is because that is what it feels like, freedom. It takes personal, spiritual freedom to live this way and allow Christ to flow through you. So ask him in this stage what hinders you from living this way. Ask him to remove those things and remember that the purpose of freedom in Christ is to **be** in Christ to be used by Christ. He frees you from sin, fears, insecurity, and the troubles of the world, and you get to walk around being his hands, feet, eyes, and ears, his representative in the world. It is such an amazing blessing! When those who have not seen, but believe that Christ is in them they are blessed beyond measure and will be shown more of what God is doing.

Step 6: Others

Now it is time to intercede for others. Lift up to God anyone you feel led to pray for today, or anyone who you said, "I'll be praying for you" to in the last day. Just a hint, if you say that, pray for them in that very moment, but also keep a list of people you want to pray for in your next prayer session." It bears saying here that for most people, this is what they think of when they think of praying. If they go to pray, they start with their list of people to pray for. But notice in this process it doesn't come until step 6. If you will follow this order, you'll be amazed at how different the intercession time goes. You have already established a deep connection to God and are in a place of intimacy. So step in and plead with him, knowing that your Lord is listening. Often, I will have full confirmation in prayer that he has heard and is answering. I find myself, again, crying during these times as I ask his help for someone, to heal, to provide, to comfort them with his love. I always ask in the name of Jesus Christ and through my covenant with God through the blood of Christ, and I ask that his will be done.

In asking for his will to be done in his name, I am asking for the high glory of God. Most of the time I find God answering these prayers for family, friends, loved ones, and even strangers. But I most love it when I know the end before it comes, because God reveals it to me as I pray in intimate abiding with him. It is in prayer that I learn the feelings of Christ and where my faith is increased by experiencing his presence and seeing him move to answer my prayers. The outcome is the glory of God, and I bless and thank him profusely as this is happening. Let me say right here, if you are a Christian and you are not taking advantage of the wonderful fact that God has made a way through Christ for you to come and partner with him in prayer, YOU ARE MISSING OUT! Don't wait another day to start trying this!

Step 7: Finish

In the last step of this prayer process, finish by praying as Jesus taught us to pray: what we Catholics call, "The Our Father." Protestants simply call it "The Lord's Prayer," but here it is:

> "Our Father in heaven,
> hallowed be your name.
> 10 Your kingdom come,
> your will be done,
>   on earth as it is in heaven.
> 11 Give us this day our daily bread,

> 12 and forgive us our debts,
>   as we also have forgiven our debtors.
> 13 And lead us not into temptation,
>   but deliver us from evil." (Mt 11:9b-13)

And then we would add, "For Thine is the kingdom, and the power, and the glory forever and ever. Amen."

Twenty years ago, this prayer was instilled in me by God during my return from an NDE experience, so it is wonderful that I get to remember that every day at the end of the prayer process. I have stuck with this process for quite some time now and have grown immensely from it. I have tweaked it now and then with certain phrases and other techniques, such as whispering, mindfulness, and silence.

Again, I would encourage you to look up Kelly's book. Again, it is called ***I Heard God Laugh***, and it gives a great explanation of how Catholics were never much taught how to pray in a way that connects them to Christ. If you would like to be guided through this prayer process, you can go to <u>YouTube</u>.

In this video, Kelly is in a church down in Louisiana with a few hundred people. About two thirds of the way through at the roughly 56 minute mark, Kelly sits down in one of the pews and goes through the entire prayer process with the church. It's amazing. I would suggest listening to the section of the video if you are starting out trying to pray in a connection with God for the first time. At night or early morning, have Kelly guide you through as you listen, and you will have a conversation with God. I bought the book and printed the process to use when I pray, but within two weeks, I didn't need the instructions.

Speaking to God in Your Mind

If you are wondering about speaking to God in your mind, Kelly explains this as well in the above video. I'll try to explain briefly here. In heaven, I know God talks to you through your mind and soul, telepathically and instantaneously. Coming back from my NDE experience, I knew God showed me my every word and my every thought when I was with him. I know now that he knows all my thoughts and is listening to my thoughts as I speak to him every day.

When you are speaking to God through your mind as you pray, the Lord is listening. Trust me in this. I also believe that when you think of someone during your day and ask the Lord to help in your mind, you are praying, and God is listening. Just to think well of someone is love, and God knows your thoughts. At times in those thoughts, you may actually feel his presence, his grace in that moment.

The Bible says, "The Lord—knows the thoughts of man, that they are but a breath" (Ps 94:11). Here are a few more verses that show how God hears our thoughts;

"You know when I sit down and when I rise up; you discern my thoughts from afar" (Ps 139:2).

"But Jesus, knowing their thoughts, said, "Why do you think evil in your hearts" (Mt 9:4)?

Here are two verses that show we can talk to him through our minds:

"Even before a word is on my tongue, behold, O Lord, you know it altogether" (Ps 139:4).

"Pray without ceasing" (1 Thes 5:17).

You cannot pray without ceasing if you have to pray out loud all the time!

Jesus Can Speak Without Words

I heard recently of a woman who had a horrible accident and was in a coma for a month. As she came out of it she explained to her husband that Jesus had approached her when she was unconscious, laying on the ground, gurgling from blood in her lungs, and blood spilling from both ears from a brain injury. She should have died, but was miraculously healed, according to medical experts. But in her description of her encounter with Christ, she said that he "told her that it was going to be okay. That he was with her and she would live." But when asked what wording he used to say this, she said, "He didn't speak. He doesn't have to." She then described a perfect peace and joy in his presence as he wordlessly communicated to her. What a mystery! But it is exactly what I expect based on my own experiences. God obviously can speak. He does it in the Bible all the time. Words are obviously important—even this woman had to translate into words what he had "communicated." I can't explain it further than that. It's a wonderful mystery, and it's a powerful blessing.

Prayer Leads to Action

Let me say one more thing about what comes after prayer. Action should come after prayer. I stated above that one of the main goals of prayer is to connect with Christ in order to take Christ into the world. Paul describes this in 2 Corinthians 5:14-20.

14 For the love of Christ controls us, because we have concluded this: that one has died for all, therefore all have died; 15 and he died for all, that those who live might no longer live for themselves but for him who for their sake died and was raised.

16 From now on, therefore, we regard no one according to the flesh. Even though we once regarded Christ according to the flesh, we regard him thus no longer. 17 Therefore, if anyone is in Christ, he is a new creation. The old has passed away; behold, the new has come. 18 All this is from God, who through Christ reconciled us to himself and gave us the ministry of reconciliation; 19 that is, in Christ God was reconciling the world to himself, not counting their trespasses against them, and entrusting to us the message of reconciliation. 20 Therefore, we are ambassadors for Christ, God making his appeal through us. We implore you on behalf of Christ, be reconciled to God. (Emphasis added)

You can see from Paul's words that representing Christ in this "ministry of reconciliation" between God and men is one of the highest priorities for a Christian. How do we get there? Through prayer. In prayer I sow a thought asking for help, guidance, forgiveness or correction in my soul, in my heart and mind and I reap a word. He speaks silently, but I translate. From this word I reap an action or deed linked with this word in my prayer coming from Christ I then sow the actions/deeds after praying continuously and perform them in Christ, through Christ and I reap his character. If you will do this, you will change more and more into his likeness. Your destiny Thy Will Be Done on earth as it is in Heaven!

It reminds me of a quote by Ralph Waldo Emerson. "Sow a thought and you reap an action; sow an act and you reap a habit; sow a habit and you reap a character; sow a character and you reap a destiny." These thoughts begin with prayer. God knows your thoughts and he speaks to yours. Learn to be still and listen, and you will hear his voiceless voice.

Open the door, Jesus is knocking. Get to know the shepherd. You hear Christ knocking, daily morning prayer is opening the door of your house, ask and you will receive; he will enter. Trust Me! Step up to the plate and start swinging for the ball. You will hit it! Pray, and he **will** answer you.

Conclusion

Love is Everything

7 Beloved, let us love one another, for love is from God, and whoever loves has been born of God and knows God. 8 Anyone who does not love does not know God, because God is love. 9 In this the love of God was made manifest among us, that God sent his only Son into the world, so that we might live through him. 10 In this is love, not that we have loved God but that he loved us and sent his Son to be the propitiation for our sins. 11 Beloved, if God so loved us, we also ought to love one another. 12 No one has ever seen God; if we love one another, God abides in us, and his love is perfected in us. (1 Jn 4:7-12 emphasis added)

I want to end this book where I began. GOD LOVES YOU VERY MUCH!

If you have read to here, then you are my friends! And friends, I hope you know by now that God is love! Life in this world and the next is all about love, because God himself is love. Can you imagine someone saying about you, "(your name) is love"? What kind of person would you have to be for that to be true of you? Well this is our calling. Our calling is to abide in God and have him abide in us. John tells us that "if we love one another, God abides in us." How amazingly simple! Our calling is to be like Christ who gave himself out of love.

Prayer is about love. We pray because we love God and the people we are praying for. Service is about love. We serve because we want to bless God and others—we want to love in tangible ways. We give because we love. We sing to God in worship because we love him. We participate in church and in the Eucharist, the Lord's Table, because we love him. Life as a human is to be all about love.

I am blessed, because I have experienced *the love of God* in my diabetic NDEs. But I am infinitely blessed because I have learned to experience the love of God in my daily life as I go to him and then carry him with me into my day. You are blessed, because God loves you and because you too can learn to go to him in love to give and receive from him in a loving exchange. It's all about LOVE!

Bibliography

Alexander, Eben. *Proof of Heaven: A Neurosurgeon's Journey into the Afterlife*. Simon & Schuster, 2012.

Burpo, Todd, and Lynn Vincent. *Heaven Is for Real: A Little Boy's Astounding Story of His Trip to Heaven and Back*. Nelson, 2010.

Kass, John. "He Raised His Voice for Tolerance, Not His Fist for Revenge." *Chicago Tribune*, The Chicago Tribune, 6 Dec. 2013, https://www.chicagotribune.com/news/ct-xpm-2013-12-06-ct-kass-met-1206-20131206-story.html.

Kelly, Matthew, director. *Do You Know How to Pray? / How Did Matthew Kelly Learn How to Pray? / Tips for Praying. YouTube*, YouTube, 11 Feb. 2021, https://www.youtube.com/watch?v=_WE3dy0HEck. Accessed 31 May 2022.

Kelly, Matthew. *I Heard God Laugh: A Practical Guide to Life's Essential Daily Habit*. Blue Sparrow, 2020.

Malarkey, Kevin, and Alex Malarkey. *The Boy Who Came Back from Heaven*. Tyndale House Publishers, 2010.

Matshoba, Mtutuzeli. "Experiencing Apartheid." *Facing History and Ourselves*, https://www.facinghistory.org/confronting-apartheid/chapter-2/experiencing-apartheid.

ten Boom, Corrie. "Guideposts Classics: Corrie Ten Boom on Forgiveness." *Guideposts*, 24 July 2014, https://www.guideposts.org/better-living/positive-living/guideposts-classics-corrie-ten-boom-forgiveness.

Yancy, Phillip. *The Jesus I Never Knew*. Zondervan, 1995.

Bono U2 Band Lead Singer Statement:

What it means to be a Christian

"We have a pastor who said to us, 'Stop asking God to bless what you're doing, Bono.'...He said, 'Find out what God is doing, 'cause it's already blessed'...When you align yourself with God's purpose as described in the Scriptures, something special happens to your life." (From an interview with Focus on the Family)

Made in the USA
Columbia, SC
10 December 2023

8d4b53ca-a6fb-4715-8b95-aaed27438fd1R01